One Path, Many Lights

One Woman's Personal and Spiritual Journey

Maria Lacey

One Path, Many Lights

National Library of Australia Cataloguing-in-Publication entry (pbk):

Creator: Lacey, Maria, author.
Title: One path, many lights : one woman's personal
             & spiritual journey / Maria Lacey.

ISBN: 9780994319203 (paperback)

Subjects: Lacey, Maria.
             Alternative medicine specialists--Australia--Biography.
             Reiki (Healing system)
             Life change events.
             Peak experiences.
             Spiritual biography--Australia.

Dewey Number: 615.5092

Also available as an ebook: 9780994319210 (ebk)

Typesetting, and cover design by Publicious
Published with the assistance of Publicious
www.publicious.com.au

This book is a work of non-fiction.

You are greater than you believe.
You are filled with a light, so bright, the
darkness fades in your presence.
You are a human being, with an irrevocable spirit within.
You are ONE.. limitless and timeless.

Preface

I have been a successful therapist and healer for sixteen years. Initially this book was written for my students and clients, partly to share teachings, partly as a memoir, and partly to strengthen their understanding of me as a human being. Along the way, the purpose became greater, and I was urged not to limit my audience.

This book is a personal and spiritual journey about a period of twelve months within my life. It is not easy to be fully honest and open, allowing myself to be vulnerable, yet I feel this book could not be written in any other way. I have learnt that vulnerability is a strength, but the first step takes courage; I want to inspire and bring hope into your daily life through travelling with me in *One Path, Many Lights.*

This book also shares channelling from the Guardians of the Light. They convey some valuable information through their Universal knowledge. I know that some of what they say may challenge your belief systems, as they did mine, but I trust you will read with an open heart and mind. Even if you do not agree with what they share, you may find it interesting and thought-provoking.

During the writing of *One Path, Many Lights* I have been faithful to my memory; however, people referred to in this book may remember things differently.

There are many whom I would like to thank but I have chosen not to write your names because you will know who you are. Thank you for your encouragement, support and being one of the many lights in my life.

Bright blessings to you all,
Maria xx

Contents

Introduction

I had just moved back into my home after a traumatic relationship breakdown and I was feeling deflated, exhausted and battered.

I remembered a student saying, "Maria you are so intuitive — how did you not know?" In the next breath, with compassion, she said, "But I'm glad to see you are human like the rest of us."

Sadly, those words had brought me little comfort. I was carrying a great load of guilt. This experience had not only affected me, but also my eighteen-year-old son and my fourteen-year-old daughter. I felt that our strong family bond had been fractured because of my choice and, this time, I couldn't protect them from the reality and the fallout.

How many times do we wonder if we are supported? I am not just talking about physical support; I am also wondering about the angelic guidance, our ancestors, the God-self and a greater Source or Being, to which I believe we are all connected.

I remember one particular day walking through my lounge room and, nearing the centre, stopping in amazement. In front of me, hovering above the floor, was a holographic picture. In full brilliant colour I could see large shining lights and a wide golden path with short thin lines streaming to the side. My attention was drawn to the light furthest away from me and, as I looked into it, I had a flashback from childhood. It was something I had completely forgotten about, yet the memory appeared so clearly; it was as if I was a child experiencing that moment once again. The huge light had been like a lamppost, a sign showing me the way, I had chosen to take a different direction and travelled along one of the golden lines leading off the main path. I remembered having consciously made that decision, ignoring my inner feelings and the guidance I'd received. Even though I had been a child, I had known.

My eyes were drawn to a second light. As quickly as the first, another memory flashed before me. Once again I re-experienced that moment and, just like the first time, I chose to travel another path diverting away from the main one. My attention was drawn from one light to another, again and again, each with its own flashback to a significant event in my past until I reached the present moment.

During that experience I realised I had always seen the signs and received guidance from others spiritually and physically, yet I chose to go my own way, making it so much harder for myself. During those times off-path I felt lost, alone, isolated, disconnected and unsupported. Surprisingly, as I looked again at the picture in front of me, I noticed I always found myself back on the main path no matter what.

I fell to my knees and sobbed. Not through sadness, but a sense of relief, as here was proof that no matter what happens, no matter what choices I make, I will always be guided back. As the holograph disappeared I felt a warm light feeling travel through me. I sensed self-forgiveness and felt supported, uplifted. My hope was restored.

Thank you, my guardian angels, for this incredible and humbling experience — another light and lifeline to show me the way.
Maria, please remember, stay on path.

Chapter One

Listening

Early one morning, I was woken by my bed shaking and rocking on the floor. It was still dark, so I quickly reached over to my lamp, almost knocking it off the bedside table. My whole body was shuddering with dread.

Fully awake when the shaking stopped, I was surprised by the silence in my bedroom. Everything was still in order. Though relieved, a lingering horror still coursed through me as if, within the depths of my body and soul, I knew that something bad had happened somewhere in the world. Wearily I rolled over and went back to sleep, with the intent that I would check it out after I got up.

In what felt like a moment, my alarm rang. I jumped out of bed, keen to turn on the television to check for any news, ignoring the twist of fear in my gut. I told myself, *don't be silly it was only a nightmare; nothing happened.* Flicking through the stations to the *Today Show* I learned of the Chilean Earthquake.

Something did happen.

Since working with Koro a Maori Tohunga[1], and personally experiencing a spiritual connection to Muriwai, a seventeenth century Maori High Priestess in New Zealand, I had noticed some changes in myself. I often felt the trembling when Mother Earth moved and groaned. Still now sometimes I will feel her pain and have found myself in the fetal position, sobbing and wailing for hours. Certainly not normal behaviour for me and, as a counsellor, if I was to observe a client doing this or sharing this information, I would question their mental health!

At noon on the day of the Chilean earthquake I needed to send some Reiki healing to those affected. I set up three candles: one to represent the Chilean people, one the animals and one for Mother Earth. I connected to the Universal Life Force, channelling the energy through my crown and into my heart, along my arms and into my hands. Holding up my hands I sent the energy, asking for the Guardians of the Light[2] and the Reiki Master ancestors[3] to assist me.

---

1. A tohunga is an expert practitioner of any skill or art, either religious or otherwise, including expert priests, healers, navigators, carvers, builders, teachers and advisors.
2. A collective of Beings from the Universal Source of Light.
3. Those from my lineage of Reiki Masters who have since passed.

Instantly I was underneath the sea. From the ocean floor it appeared as if there were mountains ahead of me. A short distance away, I saw a golden grid. The lines of the grid looked like strong rods. As I watched in amazement I noticed a thick golden rod in my left hand, similar to a staff. On the bottom of the rod was a flat round plate and I knew I had to twist it slowly, yet deliberately, from side to side. It moved easily and the sand around it floated like a soft cloud. Again my eyes were drawn to the golden grid as it came towards me and engulfed me.

In my next breath I was standing on the ground in Chile. I saw the cracked earth, crumpled buildings and people crying. I felt their fear. I no longer had the golden staff in my hand.

Without thought I raised my hands and sent healing into the cracked earth. After what felt like only seconds, I was whisked away above the earth to look through a translucent curtain into what I can only describe as another dimension. I saw souls leaving the earth, appearing as lights moving. I saw Light Beings[4] scooping those souls up in baskets with long handles. Coming towards me was a woman of around 60 years. She was round; an everyday-looking housewife with a grandmotherly appearance. As she glided past she looked at me with such amusement. I realised I had my mouth open and I'm sure my eyes were startled and wide. I was thinking, *Oh maybe I am not meant to be seeing this?* Then, *whoosh* I was back in my body and in my

4. Formless energy of light.

meditation room, somewhat jolted by my whirlwind experience. I was holding my breath, so released it with a big sigh, knowing that I could not have made this up.

I sat for a while, checking in with my feelings, then blew out the candles and closed the healing session. I got up to get a glass of water. Surprisingly only fifteen minutes had elapsed since I commenced.

As though a magnet was pulling me, I rushed to the front lawn and lay on my back with my legs and arms apart like a starfish in an attempt to ground myself. The parched grass prickled underneath but the warmth of the sun above soaked into me bringing with it a nurturing comfort. I sank into the cool, soft earth as if I was becoming a part of the soil and grass, one with Mother Earth. I closed my eyes, then, nothing.

When I woke and looked up to the sky, the sun had lost its warmth. It was late afternoon. I sat up, wondering, *what if someone saw me splayed out like this on my front lawn?* I quickly escaped to the safety of my home.

Then the tears started flowing. *What is happening to me?* I tried searching for answers then the fear rose like spiders crawling in my gut making their way to my chest. Suffocating, I shuddered and shook myself to stop it. I needed answers. *Quickly, phone Koro. Please Koro, be there. I need you, my friend.*

Koro had become my mentor and trusted friend on spiritual matters, since calling me to New Zealand a number of years ago. He was someone I had come to trust. He sat within my heart, a masculine reflection of myself, and was the person to shed light on what was happening. I dialed Koro's number in New Zealand.

That familiar greeting: "Kia-ora".

Thank God! I started babbling, sharing my experience with Koro, finishing with a big gasp... There was silence.

I could almost hear the crease of Koro's smile as he started to share his insights. I had received a huge amount of energy through my body as I channelled the Reiki to send healing. This had caused a shift in my energetic field and my physical cells were now vibrating at a much higher level. He stressed that it was very important to rest and take the next week off work to process and integrate this new energy. We talked for a while longer. As I finished my conversation with Koro, he once again reminded me that I must rest.

I still had trouble accepting the path I seemed so destined to be travelling. It was foreign to me. At times I felt as if I had no choice about the direction in which I was being led. For goodness sake, I was a practical and logical person! Yes, I was intuitive and had seen and talked with spirits and other Light

Beings since I was a child, but this had been private or shared within a small, select group of people. At the same time I was starting to understand that this was my path and no amount of denial was going to change the outcome.

However, when I looked at my diary, my appointment schedule was full. I couldn't possibly rest and let down my clients. I ignored both Koro's advice and my own inner knowing. Guess where I was going? Yes, off my path.

Chapter Two

Consequences

One week passed and on Saturday evening I treated myself to some pizza. I felt rather proud of myself. I had completed my commitments for the week, didn't let anyone down, my conscience felt clear and I was now allowing myself to rest and enjoy my treat.

As I sat watching television, something I didn't do very often, I noticed a throbbing in the right side of my neck. When I touched it I felt something popping out. The more I held my hand there, the faster it beat and I realised it was my heartbeat. Fear hit the pit of my stomach and I quickly pulled my hand away.

On the way to the bathroom, I tried convincing myself that it was nothing. But in the mirror I saw a part of my neck throbbing at least a centimetre.

My heart started pounding, I thought it would jump clear out of my chest. Beads of sweat now pooled on my skin. I felt hot and flushed, yet when I looked at my face it was completely ashen. My eyes were bloodshot and stricken with fear, imploring me, *What do I do?*

I phoned my girlfriend who is a nurse and shared what was happening. She told me not to stress, but if I was really concerned I should phone the NURSE-ON-CALL hotline. When I put the phone down, I was only a little reassured. I couldn't ignore it. I surrendered and phoned NURSE-ON-CALL. The nurse was lovely and asked me a number of questions. I was expecting her to say, "Relax and change your focus and it will be fine in the morning." Instead she asked me to put the phone down and call an ambulance immediately. She was concerned that my symptoms could be the beginning of a stroke.

As I tried to breathe, I felt my throat tightening. My stomach filled with a thousand frantic butterflies desperately trying to escape. I didn't call the ambulance. I called my friend again, who nonchalantly said, "I think the nurse is over-reacting and a little over the top, but if you want me to take you to the hospital then I will come and get you".

"Yes please."

As I jumped into Di's car, she looked at my neck and said, "I think we had better get you to the hospital."

In a cubicle waiting for a doctor I was a little lightheaded, yet tried to appear strong. Di was sitting in a chair next to the bed looking relaxed.

The doctor asked questions, observed and touched my neck then organised a portable ultrasound machine as well as a blood-pressure monitor. Di assured me everything would be fine.

The monitors arrived, as did a number of other doctors and nurses. They filled my cubicle. A cuff was placed on my arm to check blood pressure and pulse. I heard it beeping. The doctor then put some gel on my neck and rubbed the ultrasound over it. A picture formed on the monitor. It felt as though everyone in the emergency department was there. I heard someone say, "It looks like an aneurism in the carotid artery." Everyone moved closer to look.

Oh my God, that sounded serious! I looked to Di who was still beside me. Although she was trying to stay positive for me I knew she could not believe what was going on. I continued to focus on her — she is my friend and a nurse and I trust her. I saw fear in her eyes, and watched her body stiffen and move forward in her chair, which made me start to panic. You know that feeling of being trapped in a nightmare? That was exactly how it felt.

My blood pressure and pulse started to increase. I had read it on the monitor and I could also see my artery ballooning on the ultrasound machine.

Lying on the bed observing the flurry around me, I listened to the conversations. Someone was asked to call a neighboring hospital and alert the vascular unit for emergency surgery. Then another person was asked to have an ambulance standing by. *Hello, can anyone see that I am here?* It felt as if I was observing someone else's experience.

As that thought disappeared I noticed a young nurse looking at me. Our eyes connected and I was certain she saw my fear and disbelief. Her face softened. "Maria, are you okay? I'm really sorry about all of the extra staff here and us chatting amongst ourselves; it must feel a little scary?"

All I could do was nod. But I was grateful because it seemed that the others heard and quickly disbursed, except for this nurse and a doctor. The doctor said, "Maria, you will need to be admitted and an orderly will be taking you to another room, which will be more private. A nurse will then place an IV in your hand and prep you for surgery and possibly transport you to a nearby hospital. We will also place an ECG on you to monitor your heart. At this stage it looks like you have an aneurism in your carotid artery, which is quite serious, but I will share more with you once I have spoken with the specialist." He left the room.

I was lost for words. *What does this mean?*

Thank goodness Di was with me because I was feeling confused and disoriented. The new room had solid walls and a door. Another nurse came in and introduced himself but I really didn't hear his name. He asked, "Could you please take off all of your clothes except for your knickers and put this gown on. I will be back shortly."

Di helped me out of the bed and onto my unsteady legs. Slowly taking off my clothes, I felt quite numb, detached. Back in the bed I watched as Di gently folded my clothes and put them in a plastic garbage bag. The nurse returned with a bowl. Inside were a needle, tape, an alcohol swipe and some cotton swabs. He wiped the top of my hand. I turned away; I hate watching a needle go in.

"Ouch." He was a little rough as he put it in.

Looking at Di he made a face as if I was being a big baby. *What the?* My back stiffened as I looked at him in disbelief. He put tape over the needle to secure it and then left, returning with the ECG machine. After placing stickers over my chest and abdomen, he lifted my breast and connected the wire from the ECG machine onto the sticker. Smiling he said, "You should be excited — lucky to have a good looking male nurse touching you."

I was too shocked and exhausted to react. Di pursed her lips at him, which amused me. At the same time it brought me comfort knowing that I was protected. In that moment I realised how much more vulnerable I would be if I didn't have her there.

"The doctor will come in and see you shortly," he said and left. *Thank goodness.*

After what seemed like forever, a different doctor eventually dropped by. He seemed quite nice as he smiled and introduced himself. "Maria I have spoken with the vascular surgeon at the other hospital and he has requested an MRI before we transport you."

"Okay." I wasn't really sure what else to say. He checked my neck and the monitors and said, "Someone will attend to you shortly."

After he left, Di looked at me with incredible kindness and said, "Why don't you close your eyes and rest while you wait. I will be here and will wake you."

When I closed my eyes, my thoughts came thick and fast, entangled within a matrix; energy zooming from one direction to another. I couldn't keep up! My eyes opened. *Why didn't I listen to Koro?* I was so distressed I couldn't even cry.

Three hours passed and I still hadn't been for my MRI — so much for an emergency! Di was sitting in the chair with her eyes closed. I was glad someone was resting.

Finally came time for the MRI. Di sleepily opened her eyes and smiled at me. A nurse followed close behind and took off the blood pressure band around my arm. She discreetly took off the stickers and wires and unplugged the ECG. She suggested that I went to the toilet before the procedure because the dye that would be injected through the needle in the top of my hand often caused people to feel like they were wetting themselves. She assisted me out of the bed and I walked to the toilet.

The MRI room was very cold. It had a steel bed with a big round tube and what looked like something to hold my neck in place and a thin covering over the bed. The technician came out and introduced herself, sharing more information about the procedure. I didn't question anything. At this moment I absolutely had to trust they knew what they were doing. She also stated that it was very important for me to stay very still. I lay on the steel bed. It didn't take long before I felt the coolness spreading, even down into my groin, as the nurse had mentioned. Thank goodness I had taken her advice. I tensed my body, fighting the urge to move, concerned that I was inadvertently weeing myself!

Everybody left the room and I was put through the machine. I saw a spark and felt relieved that it was over.

Not quite! Apparently the spark was not normal, so they had to re-do it. *Aaagh! What else was going to happen?* I was feeling sad and sorry for myself.

Off we went again. Dye. Then through the machine. This time the technician returned with a smile and said she was happy with the pictures. I was led back to my room to wait for the results, still not knowing whether I would be transported to another hospital to have surgery.

Within half an hour I noticed a rash on my chest and arms.

"Call for the nurse," said Di.

It seemed that I'd had a reaction to the dye. Di looked sympathetically at me. Well at least I had something else to focus on as I closed my eyes in an attempt to make the whole nightmare disappear.

It was hard to rest. There was so much noise in the emergency department. I could see the workstation through my open door where the doctors and nurses were working on computers and chatting with each other. Chocolate and energy drinks were the subject of conversation and source of nourishment. They seemed in good spirits, yet they looked tired and I wondered how difficult their jobs were. Closing my eyes, I went into deep thought as I pondered the patients they may have to deal with, including the drug and alcohol addicted and the mentally ill who yell and scream at them and won't stay in their beds. Already there had been a couple of those instances that night. I thought about the different types of emergencies — work accidents, heart failure, strokes and traffic accidents. I reflected on other times I had been in this emergency department — with my young children when they'd had high fevers, stomach cramps, and knee surgery. *How difficult it must be for the staff.*

The sirens of an ambulance arriving interrupted my thoughts. I opened my eyes and looked out to the workstation. The staff were gone and I thought to myself, *back to work*.

It was 5am. It had been a very long night. A doctor arrived with the results. "Well, Maria, it seems you have a twisted artery, and it appears to be an extra artery."

You could almost feel the energy change as Di turned to look at him and said, "Where is it coming from and where is it going to?"

He said, "We think from the aorta (in the heart) to the brain."

What! You think? I screamed out in my head. *Are you for real?*

Di looked a little perplexed but this was not her area of expertise so she said no more.

"The vascular unit has gone home" he said, "and I have not had the opportunity to speak with the specialist since receiving the results. So I will discharge you now and call you later in the day."

You could imagine my completely blank look. Hours before I had an aneurism in my carotid artery that was life threatening. Now I have a twisted artery — an extra one — and they are not sure where it is coming from or going to! Even though the throbbing in my neck had not changed, it was apparently *not* life threatening and they wanted to release me.

Get me out of this mad house, I screamed in my head. I was tired, overwhelmed and just wanted to go home.

At home we paused in the driveway for a moment. Di was not sure whether to stay or go.

"I will be fine; go home. I just need to sleep and so do you. It's been such a roller-coaster ride and I know I need some time to process all of this and I'm sure you do too".

She smiled and said, "Call me if you need me".

"I will."

I got out of the car and walked up my front steps, unlocked the door and wearily walked into my home. I undressed and fell into bed. I shifted around, restless because the throbbing kept distracting me from falling asleep. I lay on the side where it protruded, but it touched the pillow with its beat. That wasn't working for me. When I changed to the other side it would hit my shoulder because my neck and shoulder were forced together. I stuck my shoulder under the pillow, but then I could feel it indenting the pillow. I sighed, frustrated, and lay on my back.

Nope … that felt a little suffocating. *Okay, Maria breathe. What is the best of a bad bunch? Alright, the opposite side to where it is protruding.* I was exhausted and soon fell asleep.

I woke up after a couple of hours and was grateful for the rest. Momentarily I thought, *Was that a dream?* I turned my head but I could still feel that throbbing. It really did happen. *Good try,* I said to myself.

It was still early, so I had a shower, just allowing the water to flow over me, grateful for the warmth and comfort as it rinsed my whole body. I eventually turned the taps off and touched my neck briefly. *Yep, it was still there.* I dried myself, not even bothering to look in the mirror as I dressed and headed to the kitchen for some breakfast. I ate only because I felt I should. I wasn't really hungry. I put on the television to distract me for a while. Hours later, I thought, *When is this doctor going to call me?*

It was about 2pm when my phone rang. I pounced on it. I could hear hesitation in his voice. "Maria it is worse than we thought, but don't worry because I haven't got all of the details so sit tight and I will call you back as soon as I do."

I mumbled, "Okay?" and hung up. *Don't worry, he says.* Well if I didn't have blood pressure or heart problems before, I certainly noticed them now. I experienced a huge pain in my chest that ran down my left arm and took my breath away. I dropped to the floor and prayed, "Please God, not now — it's not my time." Then as quick as the pain came, it disappeared. I lay on my couch to rest reassuring myself. *It will be okay.*

Time went by. The phone rang. The doctor's familiar young voice. He told me there was nothing to worry about but still there was no explanation. When I questioned him he didn't seem to have any answers. In fact, he seemed keen to get off the phone and said, "Sorry Maria I'm at the end of my shift and must go." *Dismissed.*

What? At one stage I was told by the NURSE-ON-CALL that they were concerned I was having a stroke. Then it escalated in the hospital to an aneurism in my carotid artery. Then I had an unexplainable extra twisted artery. It was worse than they thought and then nothing to worry about. I bent over, wrapping my hands around my stomach and screamed, out loud this time, to release my frustration.

Chapter Three

The Lesson

After emailing my students to cancel classes for the week and phoning clients to re-schedule, many of my students called, concerned because I had never cancelled before. With my usual sense of humour I shared my story about the extra artery, which brought on the jokes: "I knew you were an alien. Now we've got proof!" I laughed along on the surface. Underneath I was trembling with worry.

In the quiet of my home I had trouble relaxing. I was anxious and a little panicked. The stress management techniques that I knew so well and taught to my clients and students were assisting me but only for a short time.

I was questioning the quality and length of my life moving forward. I was only forty-nine for goodness sake! I really didn't believe this was my time to go because I knew in my heart that I hadn't finished what I need to learn and experience in this life.

My children were quite independent. I knew they would be fine if I wasn't around. That understanding and lesson had come some time ago: a parental rite of passage as my children had grown into strong, independent adults and left the nest.

I sat in my art room. It had such a beautiful energy and was the place I chose to meditate. Meditation had been a big part of my life for the past twenty years: personally for my health and wellbeing; and professionally, as a facilitator. I thought to myself, *Surely I can utilise my skills and continue to assist myself.* I sat and closed my eyes. Breathe, I said, as I settled into my chair. But my mind just couldn't stop thinking.

The anxiety built as I wondered how I would cope if I had a stroke or heart attack — who would look after me? I was single, my children grown up and off on their own journey. Yes, I had friends, but surely they would tire of helping me out. Could I cope with having little control and independence? Would it be embarrassing? Would I have to move away from home? How would I pay my mortgage and bills?

Question after question, scenario after scenario flowed through my mind. I could sense my blood pressure rising, my face twitching, my hands and legs unable to keep still. The dread in my chest and stomach was almost too much to bear. I wanted to scream to stop it from continuing to build. Wanting to escape from my own body, I stood up and shouted to the Universe, "God, please help me!"

Instantly I felt a break in the panic. A moment of clarity with a sense of knowing flowed through me. I raised my arms into the air and I called for my higher self to please flow into my body and help me. In my next breath I felt the energy of love flow within me. My whole body, mind and spirit connected as one in a calm and loving embrace. I could breathe ... *Oh my God thank you,* I whispered. I felt grounded within my physical body and, as tears of gratitude flowed silently down my cheeks, a sense of relief washed through me.

For years I had been taught through my spiritual teachers that you had to rise up and almost leave your body to feel the presence of your higher self and the true connection to God. That day I experienced a different truth. Yes I raised my arms but the higher self flowed into my body, and ignited and expanded the God-light within me. I felt truly one with God and somehow I knew this experience had changed me forever.

I quickly grabbed a piece of paper and pen. I could think rationally so I paused to write my next step. I desperately needed sound answers that would explain my health issues and point me towards what I should be concerned about. Was this throbbing twisted artery in my neck dangerous now or into my future?

Everything came to me so easily. I phoned the doctor at the emergency department to arrange for my file and the test results to be copied so that I could take them to my regular doctor, who had known me for many years. I could trust her and I felt confident she would point me in the right direction. *Make the appointment with my doctor. Breathe out ... Wonderful!*

I had more energy. Although the worry and stress had drained me, I felt alive and in the moment, present and aware, and ready to take the next step.

Chapter 4

Personal Responsibility

Within a couple of days I was sitting in my doctor's room explaining the situation and sharing the documentation with her. She immediately arranged for me to see a vascular heart surgeon.

A week later I arrived at the hospital feeling a little nervous and uncertain, yet grateful to be there. My specialist was running late so I had plenty of time to watch other patients come and go. Some left with a look of relief. Others did not. One patient was admitted immediately. She looked about sixteen years old. I thought, *Who am I to complain?* Still caught up in my thoughts, I felt a gentle touch on my left shoulder and turned my head. Standing beside me was a mature-aged man who apologised for keeping me waiting and informed me that he wouldn't be too much longer. I found my voice and said, "Thank you", surprised that the specialist himself let me know. A warm, comforting glow ignited within my chest. I knew this man could sense my vulnerability and would look after me with gentle and loving kindness. Once again I whispered, *Thank you.*

Not long after, the nurse ushered me to a room nearby and closed the door behind us. She had my file and asked me a number of questions, which I answered as best I could, but nothing was going to hold back the tidal wave as I indiscreetly shared my horror story about my experience in the emergency department. She looked a little startled at first. Then her face softened, her shoulders dropped and I could see a kindness in her eyes as she listened intently whilst I shared my whole story then gently stated that the doctor would be in shortly and left.

The door opened and he entered, smiled and sat down. His smile reminded me of my loving grandfather who had passed away a long time ago. He looked at my file and then examined my neck. The throbbing had decreased in the past few days; there was not as much to see.

He explained that even though a twisted artery in the neck is unusual, I was very likely born with it. For some reason there had been a shift and it had popped out from behind my collarbone.

As if in a dream my mind returned to Koro: *Maria you have had a shift in your energy field.* The doctor used the same language. Was this coincidental?

He then picked up a pen and turned over the yellow envelope with my MRI results and drew a picture showing the artery — where it was and how it was twisted — then reassured me that I would be fine and not to worry. He told me it was important that no-one place an IV in that side of my neck because I could bleed out. If that was all I had to worry about it was not too much. I was certain they could use one of my many other veins first, as I have well-nourished ones that they couldn't possibly miss.

He asked about my experience with the doctor in the emergency department. After listening, he acknowledged this could easily be mistaken as an aneurism. As he got up from his chair he reassured me that I had a very solid heart especially with what I had been through. He smiled and walked towards the door, pausing in the doorway and pointing to the file in his hand. "Is this the same doctor who wrote the report from the hospital?" he asked. When I answered yes I understood that he might have a chat to him later.

The nurse returned and, as we were walking out she said, "I'd be going home to have a good stiff drink after that experience." I knew she meant at the emergency department in the hospital ten days ago. She then said, "Oops I really shouldn't have said that." I tentatively laughed as a mixture of feelings flowed throughout my body. It was as if I was two rivers running together, the outer river flowing clockwise and the inner anti-clockwise, both creating a wave, one of relief and the other overwhelming me.

I drove straight home feeling the need for the security and safety of my sanctuary. I sat in my comfy chair and, as I reflected upon the roller coaster ride I had been on, I became aware that I had actually created this myself. If only I had taken Koro's advice, cancelled my week's appointments and allowed the integration to occur naturally. I trusted and respected him so much and yet I chose not to follow his guidance. I had not respected or honored me. I had been too concerned about letting others down. In the end I had taken almost two weeks off work doing exactly that.

The experience had also brought greater focus on me and, to be honest, this was the last thing I wanted. I had opened myself up like a book on a table in a public library for all to read. I started to feel nauseous and realised how vulnerable and exposed I felt. I whispered, *God please give me strength.*

Not long ago I'd had an epiphany when I'd realised that I was an introvert, even though I appeared, and expressed openly, as an extrovert.

I'd discovered that throughout my childhood I had developed extrovert qualities to survive it. The introvert in me loved her privacy and preferred quality time alone to replenish and re-centre. She enjoyed company but preferred to be in the background rather than the centre of attention. This was the true me — why hadn't I respected and honoured her?

Chapter Five

Present Moment Awareness

Having taken a few days to process and integrate my experience, I began working again with a renewed sense of self, doing what I so passionately love to do — teach, counsel and heal.

On a personal level I decided to never again listen to the martyr in me who feeds on the fear of letting people down. I would respect myself and walk within a space of love. After all, it was what I taught!

It didn't take long to notice changes. I felt more present and anchored in my body, and experienced a greater awareness.

After a shower I begin to dry myself slowly and deliberately, feeling the soft towel over my body.

First I drape the towel over my arms. If that feels too rough, I pat my skin gently with the towel so that it naturally soaks up the water. It feels as though my skin has a conscience because I sense an appreciation. I finish drying, and pick up my moisturiser, squeezing a small amount into the palm of my hand. Pooling in the center of my palm, it feels cool. I place one hand over the other as I slowly rub my hands together. The cream feels smooth and sensuous.

I place both my hands on my right leg and slowly and deliberately smooth on the moisturiser. As they connect, I am delighted to feel every bump and hair follicle. A feeling of gratitude begins to flow through me and I recite:

"I love my body

My body loves me

We listen to and support each other

We are in perfect harmony and balance."

I hear my voice and its soft, gentle tone as I nurture myself. I have never felt more connected to my body. Calm, meditative, yet fully aware and awake, every part of me is working in harmony. Feelings of self-love erupt and overflow like a clear water spring. I love, nurture and listen to the whole of me.

Bliss.

Chapter Six

Spiritual Midwives

Inoticed a pattern in my consulting room over the weeks that followed: a number of pregnant mums booked in for Reiki. I called them my *beautiful mums*. They warmly embraced their healing, which helped replenish their energy, and to relax into a calm state of mind and body. I aimed to help them create a harmonic balance emotionally, physically and spiritually. Through the healing of themselves, they generously gave their unborn baby the gift of feeling safe and calm. As the conduit for this healing energy, I was truly honoured and blessed to be sharing this part of their journey.

Kate had been a client and student for many years. I felt very much a part of Kate's family, having had the privilege of consulting with each member, including some extended family. She was one of my *beautiful mums,* and this was to be her second child. It was a couple of months before the baby's birth. Each time I gave a mother healing, I sensed Spiritual Beings in the room. Initially, they observed from a little distance away. I was curious, but not concerned; I knew within the environment of my healing sanctuary we were safe and protected.

I had felt their energy and sensed their light earlier in Kate's pregnancy but as we got closer to the birth the stronger the impressions became. This particular day, I saw them clearly. They were dressed in old-fashioned nurses' uniforms, which certainly took my attention!

I wondered why they were here and what their purpose was. Then they shared telepathically: "We are Spiritual Midwives to assist in the birthing of the unborn child." For some reason, I accepted their answer without question and was so comfortable with their presence that I replied in kind, "Thank you, I am honoured."

While channelling the Reiki energy, I noticed that the aura of the unborn child was expanding through Kate's aura, looking strong and easily seen by my naked eye – a true blessing to witness.

The Spiritual Midwives continued to observe and said nothing further. I understood that I was a student in the presence of great teachers. When the healing finished I chose not to mention this experience to Kate. I needed some time to ponder and reflect. We booked in the next appointment and I gave her the biggest of hugs, feeling grateful.

Curiosity kicked in. I took out the client cards for each of the five mums and discovered they were all due within a couple of weeks of each other. Interesting, but not out of the ordinary. In my years as a counsellor and healer many times I'd been presented with a cluster of clients with similarities.

At one point, within a two-week period, three male clients in their sixties with no connection to each other had called for counselling. Two of the men had been on the verge of retirement and one had recently retired. Each had presented with serious concerns about their emotional behavior. They hadn't been able to understand why they were *so* emotional and why tears flowed at the most unexpected times. They had expressed feeling uncomfortable, vulnerable and out of control.

These men had shared similar stories. They had been the main breadwinners, worked hard, long hours and in careers carrying much responsibility. Their values had been similar, in that their wives had been the main carers for their children and their households. In the past there had been no time to spend on hobbies — hobbies had been for single men. They had felt disconnected from their wives and families, their work had been their life. Yet they believed with conviction that this was their role, and they had sacrificed much in order to give their families everything they'd needed, especially security through material wealth. Fears of growing old, losing momentum and purpose in life had been strong. They had worried that their identity was falling away, along with their confidence and self-worth. Years of stored emotions had spilled over. Feeling displaced, they had been concerned that they would no longer be valued and respected by their families, friends and colleagues, always wondering *Who, and how, am I to be?*

At another stage in my working life, four women in their mid-twenties had contacted me over a period of three weeks, each sharing a story of a painful relationship breakdown. They had all experienced moments of laboured breathing, sleeplessness and decreased motivation. Ruminating about the last conversation with their ex-partner, each of the women had been unable to get that person out of their mind. So much unfinished business. Their feelings of grief had been multiplied because of connected friendship circles, shared hobbies and dreams of life-long relationships with their partners.

Each young woman had been bright, confident and successful within their careers. Yet they had gauged their success based on their ability to be in a loving relationship. A river had cut through their inner foundation, the very structure of their building, each water molecule loosening the mortar that had held the bricks together. Their crumbling buildings had caused them great distress and loss of confidence. They had questioned: *What is wrong with me?*

Each cluster of experiences had taught me so much, and given me the consistency to put my skills into practice, share my knowledge, and empower the beautiful souls who put their trust in me. There was always a mirror reflection, a remembering of times when I, too, had experienced similar emotions. The men in their sixties had reminded me of my own personal struggle for survival. Having been out on my own from the age of 16, and a single parent from the age of 33, I had needed a strong masculine driving force. The women in their twenties had had a gentle feminine urge and need to be loved, to be a part of union — masculine and feminine coming together. It had been these very clients who'd showed me how far I had come – or had yet to travel. They'd inspired me to become a better me. *For this I was grateful.*

Only three weeks before my first mum was due, I graciously accepted the beautiful Spiritual Midwives as my teachers. They were always present during these sessions. In fact, I was excited when I checked my diary for the next day's appointments and sent the reminder texts. Each day I wondered what they would share with me and if I'd be brave enough to ask them questions.

The first question I asked was, "What part of the birth are you involved in?"

They replied, "When a child is conceived, the physical process begins. The spirit is very close by, observing as the mother's physical body nurtures the growth within her womb."

"So when does the spirit enter the foetus?"

"Around twelve weeks, part of the spirit enters the foetus," they advised.

I sat up straight as I understood how we could intuitively sense around a woman well before she is pregnant the masculine or feminine energy of a child.

I asked, "Is the spirit around the prospective mother before conception?"

"Yes."

Excited by the concept, I understood that the forming of the foetus or physical body was important for everything being created in stages for the greater good of all. It made me wonder, *when I miscarried my second child at around 10 weeks, whether the spirit had commenced its journey into the foetus.*

According to the teachings of the Spiritual Midwives the spirit had not yet commenced its journey into the physical body. So many questions went through my mind. I had been brought up with a Catholic background and this was against all of those teachings, yet a knowing within me felt it was right. The memory of the guilt and grief I felt for losing my unborn child seemed to soften in the hope that this beautiful spirit had not yet commenced its journey into the foetus.

I then asked, "When does the rest of the spirit enter?" With this question I expected the *whole* spirit to enter at some point during the pregnancy.

"During the actual birth of the child, we assist the birth of the next stage of the spirit within the physical child's body. It is a nurturing rite of passage shared both in the physical and spiritual, an embodiment of co-operation between both worlds." I understood the importance of this transition. The spirit needed to be supported to adapt to the density of the physical limitations, flowing into every cell, electrifying, charging and filling whilst bringing in life. Then the cry as the baby draws its first breath.

At that point I had an epiphany. When, earlier, in my state of panic, I had shouted for God's help, I had knowingly asked for my higher self to flow into me. Was this what they meant when they talked about the path to enlightenment in Buddhism? Did this mean that as we surrendered and opened ourselves to love we released fear and all our limitations? Did we then ignite the God-essence (the Light) within our cells, allowing us to walk a more enlightened and conscious path?"

I was told, "Yes!"

It reminded me of the saying, *Let go and let God!* [5]

The more we walk in the moment, the more we love ourselves and are grateful, the stronger and more vibrant our cells become, allowing each cell to vibrate at a higher level. This expands our connection to the whole, empowering us to see with new eyes.

I had been taught, purity of love in action.

5. Adapted from Isaiah 12:2

Chapter Seven

The Illusion of Separation

I remember as a child seeing and playing with spirits. The adults around me would say, "Maria you have a great imagination." I really didn't understand what the word imagination meant, but they weren't telling me off, so I thought it was okay. Then as I got older, I was told in no uncertain terms, "Maria you are too old for this and it is time to stop!"

Our children do see and experience both worlds for a period of time until, through conditioning, a rite of passage, or by choice, they turn off the ability or keep it to themselves, like I learned to do.

Having the information from the Spiritual Midwives also made me aware of the cycle of life and death. How many times do we hear of the elderly sharing that they have been visited by someone who is deceased and speaking about them as if they are still very much alive? I believe that the deceased do visit us as they prepare their spirit to re-enter the whole, making the transition so much easier as we are re-birthed without the physical body. The perfect cycle. This reminds me of the infinity symbol. The cycle and symbol of life and death; birth and re-birth. Never broken, a never-ending circle.

Through my experience and observations, I have learnt that many people have felt separated from the whole by being in the physical body. But is that really the truth? Many of us are searching. Are we searching for the whole? The part of us that we feel is missing?

Is our purpose to know that the God-essence is within every cell and all we need to do is breathe into it? Has religion and the belief systems of our ancestors made us feel separated, scared and alone? Is it our truth and destiny to live a life consciously aware and immersed in love, rather than in doubt and fear of the next moment?

Why have we surrendered to those that believe they have the power? Are we frightened of our own power, so hold back with caution and uncertainty? Are they happy and willing to keep us in the dark, away from the knowledge that every human spirit is empowered, enlightened and will, if it chooses, become elevated?

The Bible states that we are made in the image of God. Does this mean we are God, because God is within us? Is it as simple as that?

Who are we being in this moment? Why do we believe that control creates safety and security? Why do we flow in and out of being centred and connected? One moment we are walking the path that flows from one positive to another. In the next, we can feel like we've been picked up by a tornado and are spinning in the air, unsure which way is up or down. We lose our centre. We try to anchor somewhere, anywhere, out of desperation. This often leads to forcing doors open. We create mountains that are not actually there and believe in illusions that are not real, as we doubt ourselves, allowing our fears and conditioning to drive us, disrespecting and ignoring the quiet, gentle guidance from our light and the God within.

And yet there are the moments where I shake my head and say, *What the #@%?* Is it all meant to be this hard? Is this the illusion that we hear about in spiritual circles, books, conversations? Am I creating this illusion through my fears? Is this what I need to see through?

As I contemplate, I look back and realise that every experience in my life has brought me to a greater understanding and knowledge of *me*. I live in hope that this knowledge will propel me to walk a more mindful and knowing path. I trust that I have the humility to forgive the past — the events and the people — especially myself. I source self-compassion, remembering that I have done the best I could with the knowledge and understanding available to me.

Being you is knowing yourself and seeking your own truth.

Chapter Eight

Back on Path, Mindfulness in Action

After the experience with my carotid artery I knew it was important to maintain some form of fitness and stay healthy. However, I realised it had been a number of weeks since I had walked any significant distance.

Off to the Lilydale Lake I went. Getting up in the dark and trying to find my clothes, I started to wonder, *What am I doing?* Yet after washing the sleep from my eyes I could see clearly again and realised it wasn't that bad!

My friend Charlotte and I started our walk around the lake when it was still dark. Street lights along the path partially lit our way and we were guided by the light of the full moon. It was magical.

On our past walks together we had talked and laughed, and focused mainly on our goal of getting around the lake twice in a good time. Yet something had happened. We started noticing so much more – like rabbits sitting tall and watching us. As we came close, they turned around with their fluffy white tails and scuttled away. At first we only noticed one but hiding behind clumps of grass was a whole family. A duck swam silently through the calm water forming a V-shaped wake as it glided along. The sun was rising in all its colour and brilliance. Mist hovered over the lake. Charlotte imagined we were in a scene from King Arthur. I thought we were in Scotland waiting for the Loch Ness monster to rise up and grace us with its presence. We smiled encouragingly as our imagination bubbled — something I hadn't felt for a while – and I got in touch with my inner child. A little marsupial, larger than a mouse and not as big as a rat, sat comfortably on the side of the walkway, eating happily and not phased one bit as we strode by. We looked in amusement, making up stories about what it was thinking about us. Sitting on a post, two small blue birds watched as we walked by, their vivid colour bringing us feelings of happiness and putting a skip in our step.

Everything had changed. Nature's beauty and richness was enhanced. We expanded our breath as we walked and talked, each of our senses taking in the experience of the moment. Our bodies were relaxed even though we walked fast. Our backs extended upwards as if we were getting taller. We decided to rename Lilydale Lake "Lake Epiphany" because there had been many times that answers had profoundly dropped in. No longer did we talk about getting fit. We shared that we were nourishing our souls as we breathed in the moment, aware and open.

It's so easy, through life's twists and turns, to lose our connection with the very thing that inspires and nourishes us: nature. I now understand that reconnecting with nature makes us infinitely richer.

Back in the car we wound down the windows when they fogged up from our body heat. Driving off I felt the breeze cooling the perspiration on my face and down the back of my neck. I was alive! With gratitude, I silently thanked Lake Epiphany and all of her inhabitants for sharing and showing me the way.

Chapter Nine

This Time Surgery

I was having trouble with menstruation. I had always experienced pain during the first couple of days of my period, but for months the dragging feeling on my lower abdomen, the echoing ache that would graduate to the intensity of a knife stabbing my uterus, was lasting a week, if not more. Breathing and self-healing was helpful, but the discomfort had started to get in the way of me doing things. Once, at the movies with a girlfriend, the flooding was so severe I had to leave the theatre three times. In the end I was as white as a ghost and had to go home. My periods seemed to last around 10 days — with heavy bleeding for at least five. They left me exhausted. It was time to see a specialist.

After an initial consultation and many tests, the specialist looked at the ultrasound and explained several options. Slowly, he eliminated one after the other and eventually got to the point: "Maria there is only one option and that would be a hysterectomy. Your fibroids are large and you have a number of them; your symptoms will only get worse. I believe you are a least two years off menopause and the bleeding could get quite debilitating."

I was a little surprised and was not comfortable with the thought of surgery. I asked what would happen if I didn't go through with the surgery. He replied, "That is your choice, but this is not going to go away." I agreed to go with the surgery, asking if he could do it vaginally. His answer was no. "Unfortunately for you, Maria, your fibroids are too large. You will need to prepare yourself for major surgery."

Great! Having avoided major surgery in February, by March I was on a waiting list for an elective hysterectomy!

Near the end of April I heard the postman arrive. At the letterbox I shuffled through my mail and I saw an envelope with the hospital's name on it. My heart did a little nervous flip as I opened it. The surgery was scheduled for two weeks. I had to reschedule my clients and clear my diary for a further six weeks as it wasn't until then that my specialist said I'd be up and running again. (Well, not necessarily *running* but ready to go back to work…)

After a lot of shuffling I thought I was ready. I

was relieved at the idea of no more bleeding, pain and tiredness, but was still struggling with my decision. Was it right for me to take out my womb? Could I put up with it, and get on without it? Was I allowing others close to me to guide me? Did I really want to experience major surgery? How was this going to affect my life, my business and my finances? Convincing myself it was the right move, I said to myself, *Maria you can do this.*

When the day came I had fasted overnight as requested, and needed to be at the hospital by 7am. I was a little nervous. Without anything to drink for several hours, my mouth and throat were parched. To be honest, even if I had been allowed to eat I wouldn't have been able to because of the very large butterflies flying inside my stomach. I probably would have thrown up.

Grateful to my daughter for driving me to the hospital — by this stage I was having a little trouble concentrating — I arrived and checked-in. The lady at reception was incredibly gentle with a beautiful smile that immediately put me at ease. Together we filled in the forms and she put a hospital bracelet around my wrist, saying, "Please take a seat in the waiting room Maria, a nurse will be with you shortly." I sat with my overnight bag beside me and looked around. There were another five people waiting. I was not the only nervous one. For some reason that made me feel a little better.

The nurse called. We walked past reception,

pushed through the double doors, down the passage and then into a small room where the nurse did some final checks. She was direct but had a lovely kindness about her as she went through the process. "Maria, do you have any questions?"

I thought for a moment. "No, not really. Oh I almost forgot. Here is a letter from my vascular surgeon in reference to a twisted artery I have in my neck." I handed her the letter. "He states it is okay for surgery, but we thought it might be best that you knew just in case it starts to act up." She read the letter then said, "Thank you, I will ensure the anaesthetist reads it."

I changed into my white gown and put my support stockings on. The anaesthetist had been and gone and I was ready to venture through those double doors into surgery. The wait was not long. My bed was rolled alongside what I could only describe as a very sterile, narrow bench. I thought: *I hope I will fit.*

As instructed I moved onto the bench and, yes, it was cold! I lay there watching everyone go about their business, thankful to be left alone with my own thoughts. My anaesthetist interrupted with his gentle voice. "You may feel something cold as the anaesthetic is released into your system, and ... "

A phone rang. A nurse answered it. "I'm sorry Peter cannot do another double shift — it wouldn't be fair on him." I noticed someone who I believed to be Peter look around with gratitude. Then I heard screaming. The cries were so loud and painful. Urgently, I searched for where it was coming from.

It was my body screaming. Not my mouth screaming out, but the cells where my body had been cut. I was confused until I realised that I was out of my body, floating above, watching. As I looked down I heard myself say, "I have no intention of going back in there!"

My attention was drawn to the huge male hands above my wound. I felt a familiar warm, loving energy and in the next minute I was back within my body.

Sometime later – I didn't know how long it had been – I heard myself moaning. The pain was intense. I opened my eyes to a different room, looked up and saw a nurse or orderly talking to me. He introduced himself as Peter, and reassured me that I would be okay. He asked, "Maria can you rate the pain between one and ten, ten being the highest?" Going in and out of consciousness, I said, "Eleven!" My voice sounded foreign, thick and sleepy. I remember being wheeled into another room and having a monitor attached to me. I felt the tight band around my arm as my blood pressure was taken. A nurse placed something in my hand and said, "Maria press this button when you need pain relief." Then it all became a blur.

Later I couldn't breathe. It was surreal, though I was not scared. Then I felt my lungs inflate and I could breathe again. Everything was fine. This happened several times. No-one seemed to notice what was happening to me. When the nurse came in I gently grabbed her arm to try to explain what had been happening. She looked at the monitor and reassured me that the oxygen was fine. But then I felt my lungs collapsing again — there was no air; yet I was back in that surreal place, calm and peaceful, floating. The nurse moved quickly, fiddled with the machine I was attached to and, in the next moment, I could breathe and I was back in my body. She called in another nurse and they decided to increase my oxygen. They both seemed satisfied with that decision, at least until they could speak with a doctor.

Having pushed that button in my hand a couple of times, I sensed that the painkiller was causing the breathing problems and I shared this with the nurses. They agreed this could be the case; some people do react to morphine. They reassured me that I couldn't administer too much no matter how many times I pushed it because it was a controlled dose. Still, I was determined not to use it. One of the nurses phoned the doctor for permission to give me other painkillers. Unfortunately he was unavailable, which meant I had to deal with the pain till morning.

Thank goodness I had techniques: laying my hands on myself to administer Reiki, and a positive mindset. I trusted that I could sleep through the pain, or at least accept the situation in the hope that it would ease my pain. I closed my eyes and fell asleep.

After being on oxygen for three days and swallowing only liquids, I was feeling ready to enjoy some real food, which I think meant I was feeling better. There had been no more episodes of lungs collapsing and my pain was now under control. The nurses and doctors had been regular visitors ensuring that I was okay, sometimes waking me when I was asleep. One of the doctors, a student surgeon, seemed especially happy about the cut across my stomach and how well her stitches looked. It made me happy that she was pleased.

One day I was completely absorbed by my own thoughts when another doctor and a nurse walked in. I recognised the nurse as the one who took the phone call about Peter's shift. Before realising I said, "You are the kind person that assisted Peter." She looked at me, perplexed. So I reminded her about the telephone conversation she had, and how Peter seemed grateful for her standing up for him and not allowing whoever was on the phone to force him into another double shift. I noticed she went pale. Looking at the doctor uncertainly she said quietly, "She shouldn't have known about that". They exchanged glances, but the doctor didn't reply. Instead she said, "Maria we can take out your drip this afternoon and you will also be off the oxygen." Then she wrote up my chart and off they went.

Contemplating the nurse's reaction, I realised the phone call must have happened during the surgery, not before or after. It all started to make sense: hearing my cells screaming while they were being cut, and the experience of floating above my body; the male hands above my abdomen must have been one of my spiritual guide's. Is this what they call an out-of-body experience or near death?

Later, while lying in bed, I had another flashback from my childhood. When I'd been abused I had left my body and felt so protected in my guardian angel's arms. Even though I had been able to see and feel everything happening to my physical body, I had still been safe.

While reminiscing at the connection with my guardian angel, a gentle warm breeze touched my skin, and I knew she was surrounding me with her wings. I surrendered into her loving and protective embrace. A smile spread across my face and I felt truly blessed. I whispered, "Thank you, Ashanty."

On the fourth day in hospital I started walking and loved it. It was so nice to be out of bed and moving, and I loved eating real food again. *Yeah!*

On day five I was scheduled to go home. I couldn't wait to be in my own bed. As much as the staff were fabulous, it was noisy and very difficult to sleep. Plus I wanted my own bathroom — the hospital one was communal and got a little disgusting at times.

Late in the evening the nurse came in to do the routine blood pressure check. From what I could see on the machine, it was a little high. She had a great sense of humour and said, "I'll just go and get the old fashioned manual machine. Sometimes these can play up."

Checking it again with another machine didn't change the reading. She excused herself and returned with another nurse. After another check they confirmed it was high and left to consult a doctor. I wasn't too concerned, though I could hear the whole conversation, as my room was outside the nurse's station. One nurse returned with some sort of patch in her hand. "Maria I need to put this patch on you because it will instantly lower your blood pressure. It is dangerously high."

While applying it she told me about one of the student nurses being given the duty of applying a patch like this to a patient and how she accidently touched it because it stuck to her finger — in the next minute she was passed out cold on the floor. The nurse laughed and so did I, even though I thought, *How horribly embarrassing.* But I suppose experience is the best teacher and it gave me confidence that it would work for me. I appreciated the nurse trying to divert my attention in an effort to keep me calm. With the patch firmly in place, she gently touched me on the arm and said, "Rest. We will be back soon to check on your blood pressure."

My anxiety kicked in and those terrible negative thoughts started, "What now? Why is this happening to me?" My inner victim marched in just to beat me up a little bit more. I picked up my mobile phone to check the time. It had only been half an hour since she left yet it seemed so much longer.

At last she came back with a warm smile and her manual blood pressure machine, unwrapped the machine and put the cuff around my arm. I noticed I was getting a nervous flutter in my stomach. The nurse didn't look too happy. "Maria it hasn't lowered enough — please excuse me while I call the doctor."

It was late in the evening. I could hear the nurse on the phone, but not the doctor's response. After hanging up, she came back into the room. "The doctor is unable to come in now, but don't worry we will be monitoring you throughout the night."

Great, another sleepless night!

The nurse left me alone with my thoughts. I really wanted to be home the next day — the fifth day. I could shower, and walk slowly, and my body was starting to function well. I just wanted my own bed, familiar smells, and friends and family. So, in the early hours of the morning, when a nurse informed me that I probably wouldn't be leaving that day I was devastated.

When the doctor arrived at around 10am I was determined to convince him that I was okay to leave. I didn't know how, but I was certain the strategy would come to me.

With little sleep, I showered, had my breakfast and packed my bag, ready. For extra assistance I put on some make-up, though stayed in my pyjamas – I didn't want to be too presumptuous and put the doctor's defences up. I turned on the television, sat and waited.

At long last he arrived, appearing friendly and young. I sensed he would be empathetic to my cause. He looked at my chart then at me. Before he even had a chance to open his mouth I pleaded, "Please let me go home. I am tired. It is hard to sleep here and I am certain my blood pressure will drop once I am in familiar surroundings." I was relieved to get that out.

He studied me and then looked at his chart. I couldn't interpret what he was thinking. The anticipation of what he would say next was excruciating. He then took a breath. "Okay Maria, I will discharge you, providing you promise me that you will see your general practitioner tomorrow and have your blood pressure checked again. Understand you will likely require blood pressure medication."

"Yes I promise."

I sighed in relief. *Yay I'm going home!* I slipped off the bed and, to his surprise, gave him a generous hug, whispering, "Thank you".

He smiled gently. "All the paper work should be completed within the next couple of hours and you should be able to leave around lunchtime."

Excitedly I picked up my phone and called my daughter, singing in my head, *I am going home, yeah. I am going home, yeah.* If I could have danced and jigged around I would have done that too.

Chapter Ten

Safety of the Nest

When we got home, I could see that my lawns had been freshly cut and, with the window down, they smelled divine. I slowly got out of the car, surprised by how lethargic I felt, and how sensitive to every muscle, ache and pain in my body. My daughter took my bag and opened the front door as I made my way up my front steps. At once I could smell the familiar sandalwood, rose, bergamot and lavender. I was returning to my sanctuary. The red, orange and yellow tones in my home appeared even more vibrant than usual. These colours made me feel alive and lifted my spirits.

The mail was on the table in the kitchen but I wasn't ready to open it. Putting on the kettle, my daughter offered to make me a hot drink. Although grateful, all I wanted was a glass of water and my own bed. After making an appointment with my doctor, I fell into bed.

I was so glad that I'd changed my sheets before I went into hospital. There is nothing more comforting than slipping into a bed with clean and crisp sheets. I sipped water and lay my head gently on the pillow, feeling safe and secure as I sank deeper into it. I closed my eyes ... *Dreamland here I come!* I slept on and off for the rest of the afternoon and into the evening.

Early the next morning a little walk around the house felt really good and, even though it was hard to move, my body responded well. A couple of hours later my daughter woke up and went out, reassuring me she would be back in time to help me shower and meet my doctor's appointment.

During this time alone, I enjoyed the quiet of my home and once again strolled around ingesting the beauty within it. I was surrounded by fond memories of the treasured items that I'd collected and received over the years, and felt the bliss and comfort of being safe in my nest. It was heavenly. I sat quietly and enjoyed the chattering of the birds in my garden. I put on some music, allowing the lullaby to nurture me and soften the chaos of the past few days.

Midday came and went and my daughter had not returned. I was starting to feel a little distressed. *Breathe Maria and remember she promised she would be here.*

At 12.15pm, my appointment was in forty-five

minutes, but I hadn't showered. Tears started to well in my eyes. I couldn't miss my appointment. Though I had phoned and left a message for my daughter I decided to phone my friend Charlotte, who dropped everything and was with me within five minutes. "Have you had lunch?" she said.

"No."

"Right, let's get you organised for your shower and I will make your lunch."

She ushered me into the bathroom ensuring I had everything I needed and left me to it while she prepared my lunch. Cautiously, I got into the shower and with the warmth of the water flowing over me I could no longer hold back the sobs. Tears just poured out. I was desperately trying to not let Charlotte hear me, but there was nothing I could do. I thought to myself, *Maybe I am just overwhelmed.*

Just as Charlotte and I were ready to leave, my daughter arrived. It was 12.50pm, just ten minutes before my appointment. I could see she was upset and embarrassed. Charlotte hesitated, then greeted her, gave me a big warm hug and said her goodbyes and left.

My daughter helped me into the car and we drove to the doctor, fortunately only five minutes away. Long enough to get a lecture about how I should have waited for her, and not made her look bad in front of Charlotte. She was upset and didn't offer an excuse for her lateness. I felt like a helpless child. No longer independent or in control, and feeling conflicted and vulnerable, I withdrew into myself.

When we arrived at my doctor's surgery, the reception staff were their normal jovial selves. But that day I didn't have the energy to chat. I gave a very strained smile, hoping that I wouldn't offend. In the past, regardless of how sick I was, I had at least been able to greet them and put on a great smile. Not that day.

As always my doctor greeted me with her soft voice and gentle way. I was safe in her care. Knowing that I didn't like going on any medication unless it was really necessary, she was accepting of a compromise to monitor my blood pressure for the next couple of weeks. We made the next appointment, went to the pharmacy to pick up a blood pressure machine then headed home. That was as much as I could handle for the day!

Over the next couple of days I had many wonderful friends, clients and students dropping in food, flowers and presents. I loved seeing them and, even though at times I was a little exhausted, I felt truly blessed and grateful.

The phone rang. It was my business line and yet I couldn't help answering it. My voice was croaky, sounding deeper and softer than normal. "Hello Maria speaking."

"Hi Maria, how are you?"

I knew the voice and I was delighted to hear it.

"I'm okay. I'm healing and that's the main thing."
I gave a cheeky little giggle.

My student then quickly moved to share a problem she had and wanted some spiritual and personal insight. At first I tried to help her but, I just didn't have the energy. Nothing came. Nor was I able to concentrate for long enough to focus or gain any clarity for her. After sharing this, I was surprised that she continued talking about her problem, seemingly unaware of the stress that I was experiencing.

Observing my confusion I wondered, *Why is she even asking anything of me? I have just had major surgery.* My own answer was insightful. *Well Maria, you answered the phone didn't you? You can't help yourself — why do you do this?*

After a while I realised, I wasn't sharing the full truth of the matter — that I was really unwell and should not be answering the phone let alone engaging with students in a meaningful way. Yet another part of me thought they should hear that in my voice because they knew me.

I decided to tell her the truth about how unwell I really was and that I was unable to assist her right then. Her response was a simple: "Oh." Then she paused and said, "Well I had better go."

"Okay", I said quietly, and she hung up. A little bewildered, I shrugged and laughed in disbelief. To be honest I didn't know what to think, say or feel. So I chose to let it go.

Over the next week I received two similar calls. By then, I was finding it somewhat amusing and decided to be totally honest, sharing more accurately how I was feeling. Both times I received similar responses. Though, as I really listened, I noticed uncertainty in their voices. They appeared unsure as to what to do or say next.

Lying on the couch I had time to ponder. I realised my students were not used to me being unwell, and might be confronted by my expression of vulnerability. With them I had always been the teacher, upbeat and appearing capable of handling everything. I wondered what I might need to learn, and if I had created this.

Chapter Eleven

Through the Eyes of the Child

I was only a toddler when I was introduced to the concept of *mixed messages*. At that time a feeling was born: *confusion*.

Every Friday my mother and her sisters would meet at my grandmother's home after shopping. One day my father had arrived and I'd been so excited I could barely keep my balance as I ran to greet him. With one hand, he had picked me up by my arm and used his foot to kick me clear across the kitchen, like a football. I'd landed heavily on my back across the step that led out onto the patio, unable to breathe.

After the initial shock, a loud cry had burst out of my mouth and in the next moment my grandmother had scooped me up in her arms and quickly taken me into another room off the kitchen. She'd shushed me and held me tightly, never taking her eyes from the doorway. Though confused and in pain, I'd felt the protection of my grandmother's arms wrapped around me and had clung onto her with all of my strength, wondering *What had I done wrong?*

While reliving this experience through writing it down, I was interrupted for a moment by background music becoming louder. It was a song by Karise Eden called *I was your girl.* The music and lyrics started a flood of tears.

I clutched my stomach in anguish, my mind reeling. Then thought: *Settle Maria and breathe!* I knew these tears were healing, though it still hurt. I had grown and come so far, but there was still a scar.

In grade two I had stood in front of my class for "show and tell" and pulled up my dress to show the bruises on my legs. The teacher had run to me and pulled down my dress, then taken the three-foot ruler, making me hold my hand out as she'd hit it several times. Tempted to pull my hand away, I hadn't because my fear of the consequences had been greater than the stinging pain. The teacher had gone on to explain to me and the class that I had to be punished for pulling up my dress and showing my underwear. I remember feeling confused because I hadn't meant to show my underwear or do anything wrong; I'd just wanted them to see my bruises and save me. I had felt ashamed and embarrassed, and her reaction had only reinforced that I deserved to be treated this way. This had been the first time I'd reached out for help.

My paternal grandfather would take me out into the garden. He had the most magnificent passionfruit that covered the whole fence and, in season, it would be abundantly filled with fruit. He'd weed and prune and teach me how to as well. He would show me his kind of love, which was to care for nature and breathe it in, appreciate its beauty and accept its gifts with every new season. My Pa and nature had given me the message that change was inevitable. For this I was grateful because it gave me hope.

I had lived for the moments I shared with my Pa. I would have loved to spend more time. "Why can't I?" I would ask. No answers were ever forthcoming.

As I grew up, I found I would be told what to say and do. I didn't like lying; I tried objecting, but would be met with harsh words and more pain. Still confused, I would stop the questions and become resigned. The lie had been born, and I would fear sharing the truth. I didn't want to get myself or others in trouble. I hated lying, and I hated those who made me do it.

I was certain I had been adopted. Unfortunately, later on I'd find out I wasn't, which would take away my innocent dreaming of the perfect parents waiting to discover, love and protect me.

The repetitive lies and secrets demanded of me every time I saw any family or friends continued to condition me. I'd feel as if I were in chains, denied the opportunity to express myself with my own truth and voice, which made me feel isolated in my distress, and abandoned by the world and God.

By the time I had reached the age of twelve, life was all too hard. I had been praying to God to save me, but he hadn't been listening, and the pain had been escalating. My father was drinking more often and there were more regular beatings. I'd try to explain to my mother, but she would not listen, and I was continually told I was a liar. Then came the day, that horrible gut-wrenching day, when someone walked in while my father was on top of me. My head had twisted to look, our eyes had met and I'd felt such shame. That was the day it had all become too much to bear. It was then I chose to take my own life.

I planned it well, wrote my letter sharing the truth about my parents, and how angry and disillusioned I was with them and God. That night, I snuck into the medicine cabinet and took all of the tablets I could find. I went into my bedroom, closed the door, and pulled the dressing table across the doorway as I had started to do every night. I placed my letter on my bedhead so it would be easy for people to find, and then swallowed more than twenty tablets. I fell asleep easily.

I woke up to a light so bright I could sense it through my closed eyes. Slowly I looked around trying to see through my blurred vision, thinking *This can't be heaven, this looks like my bedroom!*

I tried to sit up quickly, but everything seemed to spin and I felt nauseous. Struggling to move, I got up, every movement in slow motion. I clumsily pulled the dressing table away from the door, ran to the toilet and vomited. I vomited until I had nothing left to bring up and then I vomited again and again.

In the rest of the house I could hear my mother, sister and brother going about their business seemingly unaware of my dilemma. As I sat on the floor in the toilet I screamed out in my head Why? *Why didn't I die? Why did God do this to me?* Stinging tears flowed down my face and I knew I had to face my mother.

I sheepishly walked into my parent's bedroom and told her what I'd done. Very quickly my mother swept my sister and brother out of the house saying, "You did it. You deal with it." Then she closed the front door, drove off and left me there alone.

I stood at that closed door, waiting, waiting for my mother to come back. She didn't. Slumping to the floor I sat there and cried for hours. I didn't go to school that day or share the experience with anyone. I felt more confused, isolated, unloved and worthless than ever before.

I also loved my Opa, my maternal grandfather. He would always make me feel special. He'd often spend time in his back shed. I would watch intently as he mended our shoes. The shed smelt of leather and was dirty and had tools everywhere. I loved every part of it! I believed he also loved me. Later on when my cousins were old enough to play in the yard, he would often tell them grumpily to leave and play elsewhere, but I was always allowed to stay. It was a safe haven even if only for a short while.

Our trips home from my grandparents' house would often be fraught with danger. My father at the wheel, he would charge towards a tree on the nature strip and then swerve at the last minute back onto the road. Then he'd increase the speed, the tyres squealing. One particular night, he'd insisted on driving even though he had been drinking and my mother was arguing with him but getting nowhere. I was around five years old and my sister around two. We weren't wearing seatbelts. We hit a bump and my father drove the car up the curb and along the footpath, throwing myself and my sister around like rag dolls in the back of the car.

I pulled my little sister to the floor and held her tightly, trying to protect her from being hurt. This time I was doing the shushing to quieten her screaming and crying, frightened that it would make my father and mother angrier. Eventually my parents stopped shouting; the car still swerved and sped along the road, but we did get home safely.

I hated those times when my father drank, went into rage, and attacked. The thought of them still fills me with dread. My feelings of confusion grew, as I wondered why I couldn't remember my mother's protective hug or reassuring words.

Not long after I turned sixteen, my parents tried to force me out of school to work in a typing pool. I was told this was a good opportunity for me. Many times they had stated that I would never amount to anything. Even though I'd heard those words and part of me believed them, I had my heart set on becoming a nurse. I had passed the entry exam to get into nursing, but needed to finish high school.

During this period I reached out for help for the last time. We were living with my grandmother while my parents built another new home. My beautiful Opa had passed away suddenly; I thought my grandmother might have wanted company, and we needed somewhere to stay for a short time. Little had my grandmother known what she would experience.

One day, I came home from school and, as I entered the front door, I could see my father in the kitchen. He came towards me with a beer in his hand and, without provocation, grabbed me and started punching into me. I yelled at him, which I knew would make him worse, but I couldn't be silent anymore. Because my grandmother was there witnessing it, I hoped he would stop. But he didn't. His rage heightened.

I fled out the front door. He followed and caught me, holding me around the neck as he started to rant about how he had set up this job in the typing pool and how ungrateful I was. I struggled to breathe as I screamed back at him, and he continued to punch me. When my grandmother arrived she tried to get between us. Loosening his grip as he yelled at her, I shook him off and ran for my life down the street. I ran and ran.

When I stopped, I was standing outside the local police station. I went around the side and sat down to clear my head. Guilt and concern for my grandmother overwhelmed me. *Had he hurt her? No, he wouldn't. My uncles would hurt him if he did, and he would be too frightened of them.*

I took a deep breath, stood up and shored up my courage to walk into the police station. Even though my legs felt weak, I found the strength to stumble in through the doors. My face had already started to swell, my hair was dishevelled and I was sweating profusely from fear and the running. Through tears and gulps of air I shared my distress. Once I had finished, the police officer just looked down at me with a blank face and told me to go home. I'd been dismissed as if I was nothing. I left, feeling completely helpless and resigned to my life. I was angry as well, to think that the people meant to protect did not. A belief dissolved.

The next day, I surrendered to my parent's will. My dreams for becoming a nurse were shattered.

But, from that day, something changed within me. Deep inside, an incredible force started to grow.

It was as if I had truly connected to my spirit — a strength I felt with such power — an inner knowing that, through adversity, I had the will to make a choice. The light had broken through; faith was restored and resilience born.

Without conscious thought, I knew that a better, more suitable job would come my way. It did within a couple of months. A new health centre was opening in town and they needed a typist/clerk who would work mainly for the administrator and committee of management, but also with doctors, district nurses, and a dentist. I applied for the job and got it. Soon afterwards, I left high school.

Within a short time, a visiting psychologist named Michael came to work there for a few months. Michael asked me questions at different times during my working day. I can't recall telling him about the challenges at home. Maybe I did. But it was hard to hide.

At the age of sixteen I was pulled out of home by Michael. I will be forever grateful to him for this. Being removed from home was very rare in those days. I still have some memory loss due to the trauma of that night, but let me share what I can remember.

The front door bell rang and it was answered by my father. Michael stood there along with my aunt and uncle and a suitcase. They came inside. During the conversation, Michael accused my father of abusing me. At once my father picked up the suitcase and threw it at me. It knocked me down. As I recovered and got up, my father denied any abuse. I left the room and went to my bedroom that I shared with my sister to pack my clothes. I felt numb. When I came back I heard my father blaming me for my mother's heart attack, which she had suffered some time ago. Surprisingly, that was the very thing that put me into a state of shock. *I knew I didn't and couldn't have done that.* I was sure it was caused through too much cholesterol around her heart. No matter what had happened, I still loved my parents.

My memory of the rest of that evening is a blur. I was in someone's home with people talking around me. I even remember making a phone call to a friend, my voice monotone. That night I moved into my aunt and uncle's place, though only for a short time. It was difficult for my aunt and uncle, but I will be forever grateful to them for the courage they showed and taught me. Even then I was being guided and looked after.

The adult, through experience and wisdom, understands and forgives; yet the child within still hurts and yearns for that connection between the child and parent and, surprisingly all of these years later, I still hold out hope. Hope was the wonderful trait shown to me by my Pa while he shared his wisdom in the garden. *Change is inevitable.*

Chapter Twelve

Understanding the Lesson

An aspect of my inner child desperately wants to ensure that those around her are being heard and are safe; at the same time, she wants to be loved and nurtured and part of a family. By not being available to all, she mistakenly believes that she is letting others down, which will result in a punishment she cannot bear to think about. She still feels the pain and the isolation of her past, and has created belief systems and behaviours to help her survive. She has learnt that it is not safe to speak up and, therefore, suffers in silence. She doesn't understand boundaries because hers were always blurred. Through fear, she will often claim the power to lead.

My inner child felt rejected again and again as my own children and some of those I had allowed into my inner sanctum became distant. Guilt rose from the depths and I wondered what I had done wrong and how to fix it.

The adult me knew I had the best of people surrounding me with love and the greatest intentions. I was using all possible strategies of breath work, meditation and distraction, but still felt overwhelmed by the pain and hurt of my damaged inner child.

I said to myself, *Maria, this is not good for your health!* Then did what I know best – asked God and my guidance, *Please help to ease my pain and help me to clarify my thoughts.*

In the next moment a gentle voice intoned, "Maria you need to love you more."

What do you mean?

It then came to me, a moment of revelation: *Maria, stop putting everyone else first. This is not serving you or others; it is time to love yourself more.*

A couple of days before receiving this guidance I even said that very statement and asked for strength to carry it through. But by then I got it. I really did get it!

It is not about loving others less. It is about giving myself the same amount of love that I give to others.

This was the lesson. My students and my family had been my teachers. I really needed to understand to stop the pattern that had not served me well for most of my life.

"Thank you," I said to them, and then shook my head from side to side. Sometimes the lesson needed to be right in my face for me to see and feel. I wished it wasn't so hard to learn. It had left me exhausted.

Chapter Thirteen

The Grieving

I had been home only a few days and my beautiful black and white cat Kovu became unwell. From my seat on the couch, I saw him walking and then staggering sideways as if he couldn't keep his balance and then he fell over.

"What is happening Kovu?" I said, trying to get up. Unfortunately my couch was quite old and sagged in the middle, which was not helpful. My family had had Kovu for twelve years. Originally my daughter's cat, he'd become one of my best mates after she'd left home. His brother, Moggy, was ginger – such a character and a great friend. I had never had cats before these two, I had always favoured dogs. But my "boys" changed my perception of cats, as they had been the most loveable companions one could ever ask for.

Kovu sensed my struggling to get out of the couch. He tried to stand and move towards me. It was heartbreaking watching him get onto his feet, taking a couple of steps then flopping just near the couch. I couldn't help crying as I talked to him and stroked him gently. When he looked up at me I could see he was disoriented. I could almost read his mind as he tried desperately to focus on me and my voice. Kneeling on the floor with him, I knew he could feel my warmth. I sobbed as I asked once again for some help.

Memories flooded back. About three years ago we'd lost Molly, our Cavalier King Charles Spaniel, at exactly the same age. I'd been devastated, and still felt grief, even though time had healed the intensity. I'd loved her as if she was one of my own children. I know that's hard to believe for some people; nonetheless, it is true.

My mobile phone was on the table. Grabbing it I phoned Kym — she'd know what to do. Kym was a vet nurse and the daughter of my close friend Di. Not taking my focus off Kovu struggling and shaking, I waited for Kym to pick up. Although Kovu started to look as if he did recognise me, when I described what I could see, Kym suggested he could be having a stroke. I needed to take him to the vet.

Late in the day my vet was closed, so I phoned my daughter as I was sure she would want to know. Fortunately she wasn't too far away and said she would be with me shortly. I lay on the floor with

Kovu, my arms gently around him, and he started to purr as if trying to comfort me. For a moment I felt grateful. In the next moment selfish — such mixed emotions as we both supported each other.

My daughter arrived and we placed Kovu in his carry cage and headed off to another vet. After completing some tests the vet wanted to keep him overnight to monitor him. Reluctantly I left him. My daughter reassured me that he was in good hands as someone she knew used the same vet.

Back home we went. During this unexpected turn with Kovu I felt a shift, an inner awareness. I didn't like the feeling in my gut — fearing that I had done something wrong and it was my fault. I felt powerless. It was time to be honest with myself. I had to heal the child within, take back the power that my past had had over me, and start making the necessary changes. I sensed an objection from the inner child, an anxiety, and acknowledged that it could be a little scary for her. Taking a deep breath in then out, I said some encouraging words to my inner child: *Maria, you are safe and you are loved. You no longer need to live in fear. I'm here for you, and I love you with the whole of my heart. Know that I am willing to be your parent and I promise to nurture and protect you.* I placed my arms around myself in a warm hug and reassured the child within.

One of my students and friend, Carolyn, had made me a beautiful gift that hung in my kitchen. It was a quote from His Holiness the Dalai Lama:

"Change only takes place through action. Not through prayer or meditation, but through action."

As I looked up at it I said to myself, *Okay, well I am going to do all three to ensure the best outcome.* Smiling to myself I felt a little more energised as a bubble of anticipation quietly flowed through the core of my being: my inner child had heard me.

It was quite late by the time I had said goodnight to my daughter, climbed into bed and silently said a prayer for Kovu. I sent him healing energy as I asked the angels to wrap their wings around him so that he was comforted, safe and secure in the unfamiliar place. I then said my nightly prayer:

Dear Lord, thank you for your loving and gentle guidance, I ask that Archangel Michael please be present and place his golden shield of protection around me. Above and below, north, south, east and west of me, I ask that I be protected here in the physical as well as in my dream state and all the realms that I travel. I also ask that his golden shield of protection extend throughout my whole home right through to the borders of my property and may the land, the garden, the sheds, the gazebo, the carport, my car, the animals, myself and my home be fully protected. I thank the ancestors of this land for the privilege of living here and I promise that I shall respect and honour the land and be a good caretaker. I ask that your golden shield of protection please extend around my daughter, my son and his girlfriend and may they feel protected and loved at all times.

I ask that all of those in my life who send me kind and loving thoughts may they be blessed and feel the strength of love and support within their lives and I thank you with all of my heart. Namaste.

Placing my hands near my abdomen I was surprised it felt so empty after having my uterus removed, but I didn't want to go there yet, so I invoked the Reiki energy and gave myself healing as I allowed myself to fall asleep.

It was morning, another day, and my first thought was, *I wonder how my little friend Kovu is?* After breakfast my daughter called the vet. They suggested we pick him up around 11am and said they'd speak with us further when we got there. Surely that was good news.

So I got into the shower. Water is so healing. I asked that it wash away all that no longer served me, especially the sadness I was feeling. The gentle warmth cascaded over my body. I popped my head under for a moment but then needed to breathe. Yet that moment was long enough for my mind to empty and the pressure was released. I didn't want to get out but the water was in short supply so I turned off the taps, got out and dried myself, feeling a bit lighter and more ready for the day ahead. Maybe this was the beginning of me opening to change and loving myself more.

The vet told us that Kovu had very high blood pressure but he couldn't really find any reason for what they believed had been a seizure. Kovu appeared timid but I didn't blame him as the clinic smelled so different to home. We were given tablets to administer, which didn't make my heart sing as I am not good at stuffing a tablet down a cat's mouth especially when they are objecting. Kovu was too smart for me to put it in his food — he either ate around it or spat it out.

Over the next week Kovu had another couple of seizures and wasn't getting any better even with the medication. Even Moggy was snarling at him almost as if he was trying to shock him into getting his act together. It broke my heart. Kovu's body was hunched and he had stopped purring. He found it difficult to sit, lie or stand. I spoke with Kym on the phone regularly to ensure I was doing the right things and she offered to come over and have a look at him, which I gratefully accepted.

When she saw him she said she believed it was his time and suggested I take him to her workplace and let her vet have a look at him. The tears flowed. In my heart I knew, but it didn't make it any easier. Kovu was my connection to my daughter, as Moggy was, to my son.

I think Moggy knew as well. Those boys had been inseparable for twelve years and when Molly passed they were distraught because she had adopted them as her children. As kittens they used to sleep with her curled up against her stomach. It took several weeks before they stopped looking for her and started eating properly again. I hoped that my company would be enough for Moggy.

Di and Kym came to pick up Kovu and myself and we made our way silently to the vet. I couldn't help the sobs that kept rising out of my throat. Kym went to see the vet and Di, Kovu and I sat in the waiting room. A couple with their dog looked at me with such compassion that another sob burst from my throat. Kym collected Kovu and helped carry him into the consulting room. The vet came in and Kym left. The vet coaxed Kovu out of his little cage, had a good look at him, checked all of his vitals then said that the kindest thing to do would be to put him down. The tears were streaming down my face as I looked at both of them then the vet offered to leave me for a few minutes to decide, reassuring me that it would be quick and painless.

As I stood at the bench with Kovu the pain in my abdomen was the least of my problems. I asked, "Kovu what would you like me to do?" He looked at me. His eyes had already started to fade and I knew it was time. My legs weakened as if the weight they were carrying was far too much to bear. I held onto the bench and leant towards him. I just wanted to smell him, feel his energy and his breath against my face. Finding it difficult to breathe, he had his mouth open, and his tongue hanging out listlessly.

I couldn't hold onto him for my own personal reasons and the vet's words came to me, "It is the kindest thing to do". When the vet returned he shaved one of Kovu's arms, placed a drip in and then looked at me, saying, "Are you ready?" I nodded. It was as much as I could do.

He added the solution and within seconds Kovu was gone. The vet touched me gently on the arm and said, "You can stay as long as you like."

Over the next couple of days I noticed Moggy sitting and sleeping in the places that Kovu used to. It was as if he was trying to feel, sense, smell him. It was lovely to have Moggy close as we both grieved.

Having been two weeks since I'd arrived home after my surgery, it was time for me to explore more than the inside of my home. I needed to be outside in nature. Kovu had loved the garden. It was a beautiful garden and, thanks to a great friend nurturing it while I recovered from the operation, it was invaluable for my own healing and happiness.

I managed to walk out the front and go mindfully down my street and slowly back up the hill. Maybe I could do this several times a day? A slight breeze touched my face. It was getting a little cooler but there was still some warmth left in the sun shining through the clouds.

With my doctor still concerned about my high blood pressure, I had to get a 24-hour monitor. Not at all comfortable when the sleeve started pumping up every hour, just about squeezing the circulation off. In a couple of days I was back at the doctor. Unfortunately my regular doctor was unavailable so I saw another doctor in the clinic who informed me that I had to go on blood pressure tablets. By this stage there was no argument from me because the last thing I wanted was to have a stroke. My thoughts went to Kovu. Was I responsible for his death? Was he trying to take on my pain? I shook my head, *Maria stop it. It is not going to help!*

I had been on my blood-pressure tablets for 24 hours when I noticed a pain in my stomach, just under the surface of the skin. I pulled up my top to reveal a red lump. My first response was to touch it. Ouch! It was so painful. What was this?

The next day, back at the doctor, she informed me that I had a cyst and needed antibiotics. Off I went back to the chemist for another prescription to be filled. With a couple more days to go until I was allowed to drive, I was so grateful for the support of my friends.

The next day I noticed a slight rash on my body and became anxious. I tried to reassure myself that maybe I had eaten something and had reacted badly.

Moggy was not eating and I was offering him every type of food and fluid — all of his favourites and more that had been suggested by the vet. I phoned Kym, who told me it's not unusual for the other pet to experience grief this way.

I talked with Moggy all the time, sharing that I loved him. I gave him Reiki healing but to no avail. It was as if I was not enough — he just wanted his brother. Tears were flowing down my face. *Why now? Why was everyone leaving me?* My children were on their own path and my boys (Kovu and Moggy) were my connection to them. All I ever wanted was a happy and loving family.

Stop it Maria! You are behaving like a victim and this is the fear of your inner child. Breathing out, I reassured her that she was safe and I could, and would, look after her. I took charge, knowing that I had the knowledge and resources to love and embrace her. Folding my arms around me I hugged myself with tears flowing not of sadness, pain or fear. Surprisingly I felt warmth and comfort. I whispered, "Thank you" as I closed my eyes and lost myself in this embrace.

Moggy must have been having trouble seeing. He was walking into walls, not staggering as Kovu did, but he was just skin and bones. Maybe the grief had weakened him. I hadn't been allowing him to go outside at all. Fortunately he could smell his kitty litter and was still able to reach it.

Carefully, I packed Moggy into the car. My cyst had not completely healed and was a little tender but this time I didn't want anyone to come with me, I needed to do this on my own, and I was allowed to drive again. Driving was odd, as though I was doing it for the first time.

At the vet I learnt that Moggy's retinas had detached, which meant he was blind. It was probably caused from high blood pressure. The vet also checked my cat's heart and found that it was failing, saying that he may not be around for too much longer. In shock, I chose to take him home for a little while. All I could do was sob as I wondered if my boys had really taken on my ailments.

My rash got worse — large, red angry blotches all over my chest and up my neck. I had an appointment with a physiotherapist as part of the outpatient follow-up to assist me with exercises to rebuild my stomach muscles and strengthen my pelvic floor. At the appointment the first thing the physiotherapist said was, "What's on your neck". I said I wasn't sure.

She asked me a few questions and then we realised that I was possibly having an allergic reaction to either the blood pressure tablets or the antibiotics. I just wanted to scream! Instead, I felt my breath labouring and my body shaking inside. I knew the feeling. Fear.

Throughout the appointment my mind was elsewhere. *What if I end up in hospital again — who will look after Moggy? What if I am having a reaction — what else could happen to me?* What if, what if, what if? I screamed in my head, *Stop!*

After leaving the physiotherapist I went straight to the chemist because I just couldn't possibly bear to go back to the doctor's surgery. My chemist concurred that it was an allergic reaction. He instructed me to stop everything and see my doctor immediately. I headed straight to my doctor's surgery and fortunately was able to see her. I walked in, sat down and shared what the physiotherapist and the pharmacist had said. She agreed. I then burst into tears and sobbed uncontrollably.

In all of the years she had been seeing me, never had she seen me in this state. I only went to the doctor once a year for a check-up — very rarely did I get sick — but this year had been just too much. All I babbled out was, "Why is this happening to me?"

When she talked I looked up at her and was jolted because she appeared so concerned. Then she explained that it would happen to everyone at some point in their lives. It was just my turn. "Everything is going to be fine. We will change your medications. It's okay Maria. We will work through this together."

Those words were all I needed. We will work through this together.

At home I was fatigued. I sat and stared at the prescriptions in my hand with a real hesitancy to go and get them filled. I was frightened as to what was going to happen next. The idea of an adverse reaction and then, even worse, going back to hospital was overwhelming. I decided to fill the prescriptions the next day, which would give me time to process everything. Things always felt better the next day. I silently hoped this would be the case.

When I awoke I noticed that the cyst on my stomach was oozing, which to me was a good thing. All that stuff coming out. It didn't look as red and felt less like a hot poker when I touched it and more like a bruise. I sighed with relief. My abdomen felt so empty. I didn't expect to feel such a loss from having my uterus removed. So many questions were going on in my head. *What will it feel like when I become intimate? Will I be able to feel that loving energy within me? During orgasm, I have always felt the ecstasy through my uterus and up through my stomach and into my heart. Is that feeling gone forever?*

I started to feel angry. They had told me nothing about this. *Why didn't they prepare me for this loss?* Aagh! I took my hand away and decided to get up.

I had breakfast, showered and got dressed for the day, feeling so much better. A little more energy flowed in and I decided to call my Chinese herbalist and acupuncturist to make an appointment. I would still fill these prescriptions and start them. I just wanted a little extra assistance on the natural therapy side. I had been receiving acupuncture since I was sixteen years old and it had been so beneficial for me.

Even after a couple of weeks Moggy was still not well and looked so unhappy. It was time to take him to the vet, who coaxed him out of his little cage and checked him over. "Maria I'm sorry. I believe the kindest thing would be is to put him to sleep."

My heart jumped and it felt like it was stuck in my throat. I was having trouble breathing. I heard myself saying, *Maria, stop! In your heart you knew — please let him go peacefully.* All I could do was nod yes. The vet set everything up and I bent down to whisper directly into my boy's ear, "I love you and I am so sorry." He turned his head and, even though he had no sight, he appeared to see me. For a moment I felt warmth in my heart as if he was sharing that it was okay. "Thank you," I whispered to him. I sensed Kovu. I was sure he was with us. Then the vet turned around, set the injection up and Moggy was gone.

Driving home I opened the back door of the car to take out the empty cage. I didn't want to take the boys home and bury them or have them cremated as I did with Molly, my beautiful dog. On reflection I'd realised it had been selfish of me. I had held onto her for too long when, really, I had needed to let her go onto the next part of her journey. This time was going to be different. The boys deserved to follow their path and I needed to trust that they would visit as Molly has done and Kovu just had.

My home was empty. No cat vied for my attention. Moggy would have been meowing at my feet, gently head butting my leg, and wanting to be caressed. Kovu would have been sitting on our favourite chair, observing and watching me enter, unless, of course, it was dinner time. There was no-one needing me at all. I had an empty nest. I had counselled women through this rite of passage but was now actually in the experience. I hadn't imagined the overwhelming feeling of emptiness.

I felt grief – and loss of purpose and identity, meaning and value. For so long I had been responsible for adults, children and pets that I wasn't sure how to be any other way. I decided to clear away all of the pet bedding, kitty litter tray, bowls and toys. I put them down in the shed along with their collars, not quite ready to throw them out.

Chapter Fourteen

My Guidance

About a week after my beautiful Moggy passed, I made myself a cuppa, put on my coat and went outside. The cool breeze on my face encouraged me to breathe and ingest the beauty of nature. Sitting there, I thought about a trip I had booked to Peru. I had organised it earlier in the year before all of this had happened.

I allowed the tears to flow, for this time was mine to experience whatever I needed to on all levels — physical, emotional, mental and spiritual. I knew enough to realise it was important for me not to keep my emotions inside but allow them to naturally release. There was no one around. I was in my sanctuary, safe and alone.

Wiping away the tears, I refocused on my garden. On the far side of the yard a sixty-foot gum tree stood tall and proud. In the corner of the property was a mud brick dwelling, used previously for chickens, with a little garden surrounding it. It looked very much a part of a children's story. My garden was sectioned off into little areas. I was sitting at the top of the garden on a swing seat. This area had a gazebo, and table and chairs — great for entertaining. There were plenty of statues, crystals and garden beds filled with plants of many colours and varieties. I enjoyed year-round colour in my garden. The birds loved the birdbath, which I refreshed each day. They made me laugh, flapping their wings as they stood in the water, crooning, cleaning and squawking at times. There was always a lookout, to ensure the safety of the one enjoying the bath. They also loved the plants and bushes, as they played, nested and chatted away to each other. I woke each morning with a smile at their songs. I really did love it!

All of a sudden I saw a face in front of me. I had seen him before, and he would always catch me by surprise. I'm sure he did it on purpose. He was a Peruvian Shaman — his face was quite lined and his skin was dark; to be honest, he was a little scary looking. He seemed to be testing me. I had been seeing this Shaman for almost five years. His appearance had always been as quick and unexpected as on this occasion. Though he had never said anything, I knew that he was calling me to Peru.

A number of years ago I'd had a similar experience with Maori Tohunga Koro, which took me on a three-year journey, during which I spent almost two months each year working with him and the Maori community. I had spoken to Koro about the Peruvian man and he'd just smiled knowingly. It had taken me this long to make arrangements to go to Peru because I just hadn't felt ready for what I thought might be ahead, and what I might experience. But I'd booked, so now, no matter what, I would go. Just thinking about another adventure into the unknown brightened my mood a little.

I had seen spirits since I was little – a toddler, in fact. First had come an angel who had held me and nurtured my spirit when I was being abused. I'd had a number of spirits who would play with me and I'd felt very safe with them. But there had been times when I was scared. One Christmas Eve I was at my grandmother's home, which was a very special night for European families. We were put to bed and then woken at midnight to open our presents. I was sleeping with my sister. She was around three years old. I was about six. For some reason, I woke up and opened my eyes to see a woman standing by my bed. She was just looking at me. I didn't recognise her so I put my hand out to touch her and it went right through her body. Shocked, I ducked straight under those blankets as quick as a rabbit and held onto my sister's legs like I was never going to let go. I remember shaking with fear. I was so hot under those blankets but, even though it felt like I couldn't breathe, I was not going to come out. I was hoping my sister would wake up but she didn't. Eventually I became brave and popped my head out from under the blankets. The woman was gone. Thank goodness!

When I was sixteen, my maternal grandfather had died suddenly. I'd loved him so much and felt an incredible loss when he passed. He was one of the few very special people in my life who had truly seen and understood me. Many months after he'd passed, he came to visit me. I remember him sitting on the edge of my bed and we talked for quite a while. I could see him, feel him and hear him. He shared some of his wisdom in an effort to help me, and to understand my mother. He also gave me a couple of messages to share with her and my grandmother. When I tried to approach my mother she told me I was a liar. Her reaction was so strong that I never shared the message with my grandmother. After that day I never saw my grandfather again, but that was okay because I'd had a chance to say goodbye. *Thanks Opa, you are always in my heart.*

My grandmother on my father's side was truly an amazing woman. She and my grandfather had been strict Catholics. Though I hadn't seen her as often as I wanted, she'd become my surrogate mother. As a young child I'd snuggled into my grandmother's breasts. She'd smelt of lavender powder and had the best hugs. She'd passed when I was in my twenties. I hadn't gone to her funeral. By then I had created my own beliefs and said my own goodbye. I don't remember seeing her after she passed, not initially, but that may have had something to do with me tuning out due to a difficult marriage.

My marriage had ended when I was thirty-three, and my whole world had felt like it was shattering before me. One night I was in bed with my four-year-old daughter on one side of me and my eight-year-old son on the other side. Both of them were holding me so tightly as though they were frightened that I was going to leave as well. I held in my emotions because I didn't want the children to experience any more pain than they were already. I had been having major trouble sleeping.

I was half asleep. Even in their sleep both of the children were holding on to me for dear life. I really wanted to roll over but feared that I would wake them. Partially opening my eyes I saw a silhouette at the end of my bed. It freaked me out but before I had a chance to get up and run, I felt the presence of my grandmother. I could even smell her lavender powder and then I was back in her arms and safe. I fell fast asleep and awoke the next morning feeling less alone.

Since that night Nanna has visited me many times, and has been one of my guides throughout my life. She helped me open, once again, my connection to the spiritual world. I haven't seen her for a while but I think that's a good thing. I believe she knew that it was time for me to trust in my own inner guidance, and I'm sure she is still watching over me and will come if I call her. It is a bit like our children growing up: through some aspects of their lives, we as parents are there to nurture and guide, but then we need to stand back and allow them to travel and experience their own personal journey, as we did. *Thanks Nanna, love you heaps.*

I will never forget the pain of my children going to their father's after the breakdown of our relationship. I was all alone. I worried about them and yearned for them to be by my side to place my arms around them and protect them; yet at the same time wanting them to enjoy themselves and have them continue to build a relationship with their father. Such conflicting feelings.

The first weekend the kids went to their father's house was so quiet, and I kept listening out for them. I sobbed most of the day, so much so that I went to bed around 8pm because I felt wrung out and exhausted. But I had terrible trouble sleeping. Then I heard them … not my own children, but children none-the-less.

They were laughing and playing in my children's bedrooms and noisily banging cupboard doors and giggling. They made me laugh and gave me such comfort until I felt so tired that I called out for them to please stop because I needed my sleep!

Silence. I fell asleep and when I awoke the next morning I half expected to find both of the bedrooms in a mess, yet everything was in its place. For a moment I did question my sanity, but each fortnight they came back — I loved their company and felt blessed and grateful. They visited for about six months. By then they knew I was coping a little better and it was their time to move on. I gain comfort in thinking they were angels and that they are now assisting others experiencing grief and loss.

Chapter Fifteen

The Channelling Begins

So much had happened during the couple of months since my surgery. Hard to believe it was July already. My blood pressure tablets seemed to be working and I was taking Chinese herbs. My acupuncturist and Chinese herbalist believed I'd be off my blood pressure tablets soon. I found myself a little hesitant about going off the medication and said to myself: *One step at a time.*

I met with clients part-time for a few hours a week — it felt great to be working and of service once again. There was always such a beautiful exchange whilst working in my passion because I felt valued. Working in healing and counselling inspired and replenished me in so many ways. My clients and students had been so kind and caring. I'd received many cards since my surgery and also during the passing of "my boys". I felt truly blessed.

One day I was standing in the front entry of my home with a client and I saw Moggy outside. Automatically, I opened the internal front door and then the security door to let him in. As I closed the security door I glanced towards my client, who was looking at me curiously, so said, "Oh sorry, just had to let Moggy in". Then, bang! I realised he was there in spirit and that she may not have seen him. Thankfully she was also on a spiritual path and said, smiling, "I wish I could see them as clearly as you." Smiling back I gave her the biggest hug as we said goodbye. Closing the door I reminded myself to be more careful next time. The next client might not understand. They might even think that I'm the one that needs the help.

Moggy visited all of the time. Kovu had also been popping in. I awoke one night because I could feel him, his warmth, his heartbeat and his breath as he was lying across my neck. I opened my eyes. He was purring. I could even smell his breath. I went back to sleep so peacefully and awoke the next morning feeling the best I had felt for some time.

Then came an urgency to write. I had been writing in a journal for years, documenting my travels overseas, writing to gain clarity and to release the consistent thoughts that bounced around in my head at times. But this day was different. I went into my study and found a new exercise book, feeling as though I was at the beginning of something. In my art room, my place of inspiration and relaxation, I sat comfortably in my lovely old armchair, gifted to me by a good friend. I relaxed my body and, with pen in hand, wrote the date. I sensed a gentle touch on my shoulder, then an energy moved through my arm and into my hand. I let go and allowed my hand do the writing!

12th July 2010

Channelling: Maria we are from the Light. Ribbons of light surround the Earth. They are placed in a perfect sequence shared by many galaxies. Those light ribbons are strands of energy just like you and me. The purpose you ask is to connect all life forces. There are many life forces throughout the galaxy. All having a purpose to grow and learn from each other, but they eventually challenge all concepts within their own race to ignore the truth.

Through these rainbow strands of light are vortexes and gateways far beyond your understanding. Even in this day, 2010, there is so much your race needs to learn and conceptualise. There are many who have parts of the concept, yet have not learnt to unite with their knowledge to create a whole picture. Too many egos, too many wanting to claim this information as their own, yet not enlightened enough to understand that it is not their knowledge; it is Universal knowledge that every Being has the understanding of and every human being can search within to find. Unfortunately pain, anger, frustration and guilt continue to deny you full understanding at this time.

What if you were to throw away the stories you have held onto for many centuries through your ancestors and those yet to come? What if you felt nothing but peace and harmony? What if you didn't need happiness to counter sadness? What if you could be a part of it all: Oneness!

Are you and your race prepared to surrender to a greater power that resides within?

Know that the rainbow light is connected to you, each and every one of you. Could you give up your greed, and need for power? Could you live to be alive as *one*? Is this a practical concept that could be adopted by your race? Are you prepared to surrender your *will* to your *right*?

Many times you have come to this place and stood on the edge ready to take the leap of faith yet you have not been ready as a race and you have allowed your *will* to choose pain and suffering over peace and harmony. We understand, for we are the Guardians of the Light. We understand your apprehension and desire to live a *limited* life. We understand you are more than you see. We understand that you have choice through *will*.

Maria: So what is our role here on Earth?

Channelling: You ask and yet you are not listening! Do you really want to hear, young one?

Maria: *Now my ego has kicked in.* Am I a young soul?

Channelling: So quickly you divert from the energy of knowing, so quickly you flow back into your story, your limitation, your mind.

Maria: You're right!

Channelling: It is not about being right or wrong, my child. It is about asking the right questions and then waiting to listen to the answers.

Maria: Okay, so what is our purpose here on Earth?

Channelling: Well done! We shall now share the knowledge with you so that you may share with many. Breathe, listen and notice how your mind distracts you from what you can hear. How can you hear or listen to us when you are thinking? Breathe.

Earth was meant to be a playground for many Light Beings. You have heard of the concept "Heaven on Earth?" This is exactly what Earth was meant to be. Mother Earth is an organism — a star light. She was meant to nurture and provide the density for these Light Beings to share and be able to live. Your kind talks about aliens, a sad concept to us because we are only "alien" due to the changes unpredicted by Mother Earth and the Council of Guardians.

The Light Beings lost their connectedness to the Oneness and started the search to find it. Through this separation they lost their knowing, and isolated themselves, eventually creating a side not expected nor foretold by the Guardians. They embraced *will* with an almighty strength and power and chose to use this power to destroy Mother Earth and themselves. The rainbow light around Mother Earth has protected her from dissolving, yet has not stopped the deterioration and tiredness she feels when she is not respected or supported.

You are not being punished by being on Mother Earth. You need to understand that this is a privilege. Your purpose has never been anything more than to *live* and *be* in peace and harmony. Yet you don't trust this message!

Maria: How can we surrender our *will*, yet not feel like we lose everything, even though you say we would gain?

Channelling: You have regressed, my child. What do you have to give up? Limitation! Fear, sadness, power, control. Breathe and listen. Your mind has gone off again. See how easily you choose to be distracted. See how easily you waste your energy and your connection.

I sat in my chair, wondering what had just happened. I could feel the energy moving my arm and the writing in the book was not mine. I wrote urgently to get this information down. I actually felt quite buzzed and interested in what was being written. On one level it seemed right and true. I decided to sit again the next day.

13th July 2010

Channelling: Maria welcome to "learning class".

Maria: What do you mean?

Channelling: Many moons ago on another planet existed a school of learning. Here were the teachers of many life forms sharing their knowledge to create a Universe filled with peace and harmony. This knowledge was shared so that no life form had power over another. Each race knew everything, each race rose to the challenge to create many worlds filled with peace and harmony. Each race was equal.

Maria: Sorry but this sounds too sweet and a little bit like a fairytale?

Channelling: Okay, let's begin. Are you prepared for this? Maria is your name. Spell it backwards.

Maria: Airam... Don't understand?

Channelling: What is in a name? It is only words put together by letters. It is not your name that identifies you; it is the energy surrounding your name. It is the energy that creates the motion.

Chapter Sixteen

Moving Forward

A couple of months after my operation, my health seemed to be going well and I was back working full time and loving it. I was still a little on edge, especially when I felt a niggle within my body, but I was using techniques to ensure that my anxiety didn't create more than what was really happening.

During this time my doctor mentioned that she hadn't experienced someone as aware of their body as me. I felt good about that because I have a strong belief in the connection between body, heart, mind and spirit, and I was aware that in the past, strong emotions within me had created small physical ailments — psychosomatic responses to stress. When I stop and listen I actually know what I need to do to bring myself back into harmony. When I ignore the signs I very quickly have to deal with the consequences.

But a couple of months after the operation I was getting a lot of pain in the right side of my abdomen. With only one week remaining before my trip to Peru, I decided I'd better get it checked out. My surgeon phoned the radiology department and arranged for me to see them that day. I was delighted by his fast response, yet at the same time, my anxiety reared up like a wild horse that had been spooked.

The horse whisperer within me quickly calmed it down. Though its nostrils were still flared and its breathing was heavy I could see its eyes clearly connecting with mine as we both gently surrendered to this moment. I breathed out, reminding myself that everything would be OK.

Busying myself around the home, I threw a few things in a pile near my empty suitcase. I smiled at the memory of my first overseas trip on my own. I'd had my suitcase packed one month before I left and had needed to go into that suitcase a number of times to get clothes to wear and then re-pack them. I should have saved myself the trouble and done what I have since learnt to do — have everything clean, a list written and permission not to work the day before I leave so I can pack and do any final shopping. It creates less stress. My trip to Peru was also different, as I didn't have to put my "boys" into care. Thinking of them brought tears to my eyes and pain to my heart. I took a deep breath in and out. My eyes became less cloudy and the tears subsided. I missed them.

Driving to the radiology department the radio was on and the music had a great beat, which put a smile on my face. I turned it up and sang along. Laughing, I knew I was distracting myself but sometimes that's a good thing!

At radiology, there was a park waiting for me and I thanked my angels. Secretly I had whispered to the angels to arrange a car park because I knew this was a busy place ... I was beginning to understand that if we need help all we need to do is ask.

I was to undergo an external and internal ultra sound, a little uncomfortable but well worth it as I didn't want any problems in Peru.

The radiologist could see that my right ovary had just ovulated. She couldn't quite find my left ovary but I wasn't too concerned because it was the right side that had been giving me pain.

When it was all finished she left so I could get dressed and clean up the gel she had put all over me. At reception I paid a fee, a little higher than I thought, but my health and peace of mind were certainly worth it. I was informed that they would fax the report to my surgeon and I would need to get the results from him. That was OK. My surgeon had said he would call me later that afternoon with the results. I was out and about so it was a good opportunity for me to grab a few things for my trip and then go home to do some work.

I hadn't been home long when my mobile rang. It was my surgeon, who kindly shared that all was well and he believed that the pain was caused by my first ovulation since the surgery. That was possibly why I'd felt it so much. I was relieved to hear him say that I was fine to travel to Peru and to have a wonderful holiday.

"Thank you God," I whispered. "And thank you to my surgeon for being an incredible person who responded immediately and came through for me."

I felt incredibly grateful, blessed and especially supported because I knew that I needed to go to Peru and I had to believe that the Shaman had been calling me for a reason. Mind you, through my past experiences I had learnt to travel without expectation and to expect the unexpected. To date I have never been disappointed.

When I had booked my trip to Peru I'd known I had to go to Lake Titicaca. That was the most important place for me to travel to and I needed to go for at least three weeks. I'd also chosen Machu Picchu. Because it was such an iconic destination it would have been remiss of me not to experience it. However, when I remotely connected energetically to Machu Picchu, I didn't feel like much of the old energy was still there. Oh well, I would find out soon! A couple of my colleagues had been a little horrified at how little research I did when visiting a country and how little interest I had in the details of the tour. I have to admit I really don't like details and on these spiritual journeys I just know that whichever tour company, destination, accommodation and new people I will meet will be perfectly in line with my learning and experience. I really do trust.

I love to meditate daily as it gives me the opportunity to connect to my inner guidance and to keep myself centered and aligned. Normally I would go to my art room and sit in my big comfy chair but today I wanted to lie on my couch. I had a lovely blanket over me to keep me warm, cozy and comfortable.

I closed my eyes and asked for the Guardians of the Light to encircle me, above and below, north, south, east and west of me. *Please protect me at all times as I open with love knowing that whatever insight or experience I have it will be guided by the light. Thank you.*

I took a couple of deep breaths in and out and then allowed my breathing to flow naturally to its own rhythm. My body began to relax. My mind cleared and then … I saw myself flying through the sky over landscapes I had never seen before. Slowing down to take in the view I could see beautiful lush greenery below. There were pictures on the ground, like children's drawings. In the next moment I was on the ground walking … I was in a maze and walking on the actual lines of these drawings. The word "nascar" came to me and, as I pondered that word, a ripple of energy flowed through me. I was open as if a flower was unfolding within. The energy was familiar, yet ancient and well before my time. From then onwards, I didn't know what was happening. Maybe I fell asleep. Yet I do remember hearing myself breathing softly, aware of the sounds in my home and outside my home. When I came back into full awareness I was re-energized. Then I heard the word "nascar" again.

Sitting up I grabbed my glass of water to sip and wonder. *What does this mean?* I knew of nascar racing teams as a sport. Maybe I needed to search the internet to find out. Just love Google! When I typed in "nascar" the first thing that popped up was "adventures in Peru". There was a picture of what looked like an eagle to me etched into the ground, but something was not right — it was desert not the lush greenery I had just experienced in my meditation. I wondered, *Does my tour take me to the Nazca lines?*

I quickly went to my folder with my trip details in it, and yes I was indeed visiting the Nazca lines as well as flying over them in a small plane. Pondering for a minute I wondered about the significance of this meditation. Would this be another place that I would experience something profound?

I sat and read through my whole itinerary and became really excited about my journey — it seemed as though it was going to be a real adventure. I giggled to myself and experienced that familiar feeling of delight, knowing that once again I was being led and supported to go where I need to be. *Thank you, thank you, thank you,* I whispered then got up feeling eager for the first time since booking the trip. It was full steam ahead.

In Peru, on our way to Puno and Lake Titicaca, many in the group were starting to feel the altitude. We had just visited the Sillustani Funeral Towers, which was over 4000 meters above sea level and one of the guys on the trip was quite ill. We had to make an unexpected stop in a local town.

We got off the bus and I was outside having a good stretch. I wasn't aware of a mature-aged Peruvian man coming towards me until he was right in my face. He stood and spoke to me in his own language for what felt like a number of minutes and then turned and walked away, giving me quite a shock I must say. Others from the tour close by looked as startled as I was. I shook my head with amusement as I watched him walk down the street.

Ten minutes later I looked to my right to see him standing only a couple of meters away, smiling at me. Our eyes connected and I thought to myself: *I know him,* and then he vanished. I didn't think anything further of it.

Soon we arrived at Lake Titicaca, got into a boat and enjoyed a scenic tour across the lake. We stopped to visit the people living on the floating reed islands, and learnt that every three months they have to rebuild their homes and, sometimes, have to create another island.

On Taquile Island we visited a community of two thousand involved in sustainability. We walked up the hill, had lunch and spent some time with local men knitting the most beautiful garments. But I sensed I had to leave the group, so I walked back down and along the shoreline. It was quite rocky. I took off my shoes and socks and walked into the lake, raised my hands and sang. Muriwai the seventeenth century high priestess often channelled through me, and her voice was mesmerising. As she was singing, I could see a strand floating to my right that was connecting Lake Titicaca to Lake Taupo in the North Island of New Zealand. It was a union of the ancestors, and I was the vehicle to connect them. Muriwai finished by placing our hands in the water.

Standing there for a while, I heard my name being called. The others had already boarded the boat and were waiting on me. I quickly, though awkwardly, got out of the water, grabbed my shoes and socks and manoeuvered over the rocks to the boat.

That night I realised I had met my Shaman that very day at the unexpected stop and, of course, we met exactly as it had been playing out at home. Momentarily, I felt a sense of disappointment that I didn't get the opportunity to really sit and talk with him, yet there was a knowing within that it was okay, and that whatever he said would come to me when I was ready to hear it.

I have wondered whether the ritual Muriwai and I did on Lake Titicaca had something to do with him. Surprisingly, I have never seen him again.

Chapter Seveteen

Further Insight

17th November 2010

Maria: I'm so sorry for resisting and waiting this long. I'm not sure whether you are my teachers sharing knowledge to assist me further in my own personal teaching with my students, or you want me to write a book to be published to share the teachings. I suppose I am asking: is it you that has stopped my computer and internet to encourage me to write?

Channelling: Maria, see what we see. See what you feel seeing what you see. In answer to your question, do you believe in love? Do you trust love? Do you connect to all that is through your dreams and are you connected to us through your spirit? What do you believe? Haven't we proven to you many times that we are guiding and protecting you? Do you believe enough to trust this writing in this moment? Why do you question? You already know the answer. The book will be one of five. You must spend the time with us to receive the information. We will not push you, yet will continue to believe in you. Please do not question your truth and abilities. You are one of us and have been forever with us. The world is changing and there is more to do. Share your knowledge and your experiences, as many have been grateful for your knowledge. Allow the blessings of your experiences to penetrate. Allow the movement of your life to touch others. Know that there is purpose to everything that is happening right now.

Maria: Okay. I will be disciplined and make the time to write. Thank you. By the way, are you behind the electrical challenges in my home?

Channelling: Yes! Are you surprised?

Maria: No. Okay, let's get started again.

Channelling: Belief comes through experience feeling emotion.

Maria: Is that me taking over again?

Channelling: Yes and no... Breathe. Belief is an emotion attached to experience. Maria, let's start again tomorrow.

I was having trouble letting go completely and allowing the guidance to channel and utilise my arm to get the ideas and truths onto the page. I was annoyed at myself and unhappy that the Guardians of the Light had cut it off so quickly. It was time to go and do something else, hoping that tomorrow I would find a way that would work for all of us.

The next day, I decided to sit and meditate first to ensure that I was aligned with myself and the task at hand, and settled into my chair. I wanted to ask for insight into the dilemma I had with relinquishing control as they use my arm to write. There must be a simple solution. Ensuring that my back was straight, I propped myself up using a cushion, with my feet firmly on the ground.

Ready, I took a deep breath in and then a longer breath out. My body slowly relaxed and sank into the chair. It was like the body knew the routine and immediately responded as soon as I took that first breath. My thoughts stopped and I felt a sense of peace. The pressure I had felt in my head earlier had released. I checked throughout my body to see if there was any resistance or whether anything was uncomfortable. No. My body and mind were working in harmony.

My breath flowed silently and without effort. There was a little pressure in my third eye as it opened and I saw the most beautiful golden colour then violet and then the colours seemed to dance with each other as if looking through a kaleidoscope. My whole body experienced a wonderful lightness like it was no longer there. Simultaneously, feelings of joy and bliss erupted, as I became the colours swirling and dancing happily and freely within the Universe.

I became aware of the warmth within my heart and the answer came to me: "Maria we can work together. We will happily say the words as we write them using your arm and hand. There is no need to struggle for we love you." My thinking mind came alive and the practical me responded, "Yes that will work, thank you."

Becoming more aware of my body in the chair, I could feel cool air entering through my nostrils. I opened my eyes, excited to start. I stood up and took my exercise book and the blue pen out of my drawer. I had to use this particular colour and type of ballpoint pen each time. I sat back down and wrote the date.

18th November 2010

Channelling: Maria, see what you can see, see what you are in this world. Live like you do, Maria. See yourself through your soul's eyes and really see. Let's begin.

Keeping with what we have shared so far — light is energy moving the energy of seeing energy, observing seeing through many beams of energy.

Maria: Doesn't make sense to me.

Channelling: See energy through energy. Some energy is represented by light. Light is seen through the many prisms of ever-changing movement within our Universal structure. There must be structure to assist energy to form. A long time ago when the Universe was created, there was very little of anything, meaning: no form. Seriously, energy is an energy, seeing energy.

Maria, how are you feeling with your role? Have you accepted your destiny? Do you understand the importance of what is taking place? Thank you for taking the time to connect.

I stopped writing. The words "destiny" and "role" floated around in my head. What were my beliefs? Did I believe in destiny? Did I believe that each person has a role to play in the fabric of our Universe? I pondered this for a while and really couldn't come up with a definitive answer. I knew that, even as a young child, I would stare out to the stars. I knew I was "star child" and that my role was to inspire hope in the world. Surprisingly, as a child I never thought to question. As an adult, I wondered: *Am I worthy?*

Channelling: Maria, you are now seeing what has been seen before by many who have chosen this path. Since time was created, we have shared information.

29th November 2010

Channelling: Maria, we see many things moving in time throughout the Universe. Time, not as you understand yet, moving in threads through many space continuums, each thread continuing to be a part of the one. It appears like many separate threads, yet this is an illusion created through the spectrum of how the Universe appears to the human eye. Your scientists are now working this out through quantum physics. Everything is happening simultaneously — your cellular structure is no different. Through much work you can heal yourself. Why? For you are a part of this thread. This thread is continuous and cannot break or die. When the physical body stops functioning your cells continue to evaporate into the energy of your spirit, as you say, yet you are just energy — a part of much more yet no less than you dream about. This energy taps into the Oneness and downloads your experiences from this Earth plane, assisting the whole to continue to create a library of knowledge. The library is available to all Beings of Light for we are one. Yet some choose to hold onto their life as it was on the Earth plane and need assistance to accept that they are ONE, and no longer need to hold onto what was and what will be. There is no need for free will for we are free.

I thought to myself: *Our free will is no longer required within this space continuum. We become ONE with the Universal stream of light. No longer separated, no beginning and no end. Merged with God.*

1st December 2010

Channelling: Many say that you are but Oneness. Many say that you are many cells creating many lives. Many say that the Universe is expansive. Many say that the world is existing love.

Maria: That doesn't make sense to me.

Channelling: Maria, nothing makes sense for there really is no answer to your questions of existence. For everything is everything. There is no time as you see it. There is no separation. There is nothing to search for except to accept the present existence for the gift that it is. You have seen some unexplainable things in your photos of late. Don't you think, through expanding your awareness that you are seeing so much more, and that so much is now synchronistically working with you? You are seeing Light Beings!! You are seeing prisms of light. These are reflections.

Maria: Of What?

Channelling: Lucky we have a sense of humour. Reflections of your past, present and future. These are what they are. Memories!

Maria: What do you mean by memories?

Channelling: Notice the colour last night, the pink orb as you call it. You are getting closer to accepting love into your life and he has been here before — you are meeting through the vortexes.

Maria: I still don't completely understand.

Channelling: Believe. Allow your heart not your head to connect to what we are saying. The more you open to love the greater you will see that everything is a reflection of you. Even the separation is seen through your eyes, yet the beauty is being felt through reconnecting to the thread of Oneness. You are opening, my child, to a greater way of being. Far greater then you could ever imagine.

Maria: Thank you I am feeling it within me as we write together in this moment. A beautiful calm warmth is flowing as my heart opens like a lotus emerging through the muddy water and moving towards the light, pure and uninhibited, a true connection to love!

Channelling: How the true energy flows. How the light sees all through so little. We, the Guardians of the Light, see through the little obstructions that you and many others place around themselves to hide their light and beauty. This takes energy and drains you. Why would you choose to stay in this state?

Maria: I agree and understand in this moment but unfortunately through conditioning, beliefs and experiences I have learnt that it is not safe to show your light and stand in your power. The fear of being really seen and exposed can be paralysing, so the walls come up to protect against vulnerability; to ensure that I am safe and do not get hurt. This has helped me survive throughout my childhood, but now I realise I have carried it within my subconscious. I've created a part, which had emotions and beliefs. This was the survival mechanism, the behavior that walked me right into experiencing Groundhog Day through many relationships, and I have wondered why it was still happening to me.

I think I understand. My survival mechanisms were needed at the time of the event, but are now holding me back. It's time to give that part another role. One that is worthy of who I have become, the woman who gained insight and wisdom from those events, and has found compassion and understanding for herself and others. Thank you for challenging me. I have looked at this intellectually before but I don't think I'd allowed it to penetrate the shell that I so resourcefully created. Thank you.

3rd January 2011

Channelling: Maria, see what we see, seeing all. See what we are through the Universal eye. See what is only an illusion of thoughts seeing you in this moment. See the structure of your thoughts as they create your illusion. There is so much to share, yet it is simple if you can clear your thoughts and become one with us.

Many have seen before. Many have shared before, yet now is the most crucial time for you to acknowledge your inner Source. Connect to the library of knowledge — how else do so many see what is possible? Where does faith begin? Where does faith end? How do you recognise the endings and beginnings? How do you share love? What is love? Is it physical? Is it emotional? Is it spiritual? See how limited you have become. See how you categorise everything. Why do you feel the need to analyse? Why is this necessary and why do you make it so complicated? There is no need to complicate anything. Look within. Feel the cells in your body — they are alive and filled with life. The idea that we need to explain ourselves is limited thinking. Young ones each day share the knowledge with you through their innocence. They are more connected to the Rainbow Light. They have not yet learnt to question their existence. They are more accepting. Many of you are awakening because it is timely. The shadow within is slowly fading and the light is illuminating.

Yes, there are forces that would like you to remain shackled to your self-imposed limitations. Yet the light within is growing stronger and, as you accept and acknowledge the simple truth, these forces will have no power over you.

See the truth! Accept the light and be bright. Do not fear for, there is nothing to fear! Allow the energy of love to penetrate. Alter your thinking — love does not come from outside of yourself and it is not something you purchase. It is who you are. It is your truth. It is within. Your thoughts keep you from feeling connected. Your thoughts create your experiences. Your thoughts separate you from your truth. You are a Being of Light. You are Source. You are light and dark! You are yet to understand the wholeness of the Universe. Feel the space you create around you. Now connect, close your eyes and look within. Notice there is no space separating you physically. Go further within and flow through your cells. Feel the emotion within these cells. Sense. Do not attach and judge, just sense and feel. Now go further into your heart centre, flow into the light held within each and every cell. Be the light. See yourself expanding; sense the light expanding through you. Open your eyes and allow the light to flow through your eyes. Know that you are connected to everything in your sight. Everything is illuminating as you become fully connected and alive in the Oneness. Hold this moment.

Maria: I can feel that expansiveness. I can feel that connection and the colours are so intense and vibrant, much more than I have consciously experienced before. Thank you.

4th January 2011

Channelling: Let the knowledge of love remove the fear. Let the knowledge set the intention to see all that is within. You are now seeing not through thought or sight. You are seeing through the openness of love's everlasting strand. See the energy flow through you, connected to all that is, and what will ever be. Allow thoughts to disappear as you accept your truth in this moment. Allow thoughts to disappear into the everlasting strength of love and light, the gift of the Universal stream. You are questioning, aren't you, the relevance of what we share.

Open, my children, for you are in the presence of greatness. Ours! For we are the Guardians of the Light. We are pleased to be in your presence. We are guiding you all to see your greatness. Do not allow your thoughts to limit you in this moment. Allow yourself to believe, feel and accept. We are here to assist you to see what many have seen before. Yet many of these Beings of Light did not embrace or understand until they left the Earth plane.

We talk to you through your daydreams. We share with you through the grace of nature and we warn you through the rumblings within your Being. Sit not in judgment. Sit not in deep thought and analyse our words. Connect through your heart and allow the truth to set you free. Do not despair, for you cannot die! Do not restrict, for you cannot fly. Do not believe what your governments have fed you. For they live in the fear of a free world. They live in fear of peace and harmony. They live in fear of losing their power. In the end they have no real power for as each soul passes they remember and momentarily regret. Yet there is no judgment, there is only learning and hopefully one day soon you will relinquish control and set yourselves free through claiming your RIGHT to be FREE.

5th January 2011

Channelling: Maria, see the signs that we are within the service of the seeing sight. See the signs now as we move you to see. See the signs as you are working through your thoughts of unworthiness. See the signs for we are supporting you in this project. Trust that you will be safe and secure. Trust that you have been chosen to write this book for a reason. You have the ability to see and feel us. You have the ability to communicate authentically to the world. You are one of five who will complete these books. All books will share much knowledge and all books will be divinely channelled.

Take heart, child of the light — you are not alone. You are fully supported both on the Earth plane and through the Universal energy. Take heart and trust. Allow the will of the whole to work through you with grace. Allow your will to surrender to the will of the light for we are working tirelessly to bring the message to many. There is so much being done to assist you all to raise your vibration so that you may all see and then feel the energy of love coursing through each and every cell. We will always support you for you are us and we are you, fully connected in this moment — past, present and future.

Many have felt the gift of love fleetingly yet have been unable to sustain it, believing that it is a gift that, once unwrapped, is no longer valuable. Then they concentrate on the future pain and past pain of lacking. Uncertainty. Breathe and connect to the energy moving through you. Feel your feet on the ground and allow yourself to be in this vibration. Observe the energy in your feet, consciously fill up your lungs with each breath and then breathe out. How simple yet so important. Trust your breath. Trust your feet. Trust your observations. Your spirit is within every cell of your Being. You are a light like no other. You are an organism made through much discovery. You have never been disconnected from us for you are a part of everything in this Universe.

Maria: So this book is about trust, surrendering and belief in our inner connection to the whole?

Channelling: Yes, and yet there is so much more because your race has had thousands of years in fear, believing you have no choice and surrendering your power to the will of others. You will need and require further understanding. Let us begin with the world you live on. Mother Earth is a living organism — she is a star. She breathes, exhales, moves, thirsts and sheds, yet at all times supplies you with food, water, shelter, beauty.

Maria: My thoughts have just come in and are influencing this writing.

Channelling: Yes they have — time to rest.

I was speaking with one of my students and shared some of what the Guardians of the Light had channelled. It was interesting the way she interpreted what they were saying. She was defensive about having to live in this world saying that we need a home to live in, money to survive and a job to give us all of that. She was angry because she thought that by surrendering her will, she would have to give up her right to live a happy and fulfilled life with comfort, security and abundance financially, physically and emotionally.

In that moment I realised what the Guardians of the Light had been sharing. It is our right to create an abundant life for ourselves and our community. When we surrender our *will* to love and the *whole,* the ego, with its limitations, fear and force has no power in this space. Our inner and outer worlds will reflect the beauty, peace and harmony we all so desire and feelings of comfort, warmth and connection will fill us. We will no longer be empty and will stop searching for what is missing.

As I sat writing, my eyes were drawn to a piece of artwork on the easel that I had drawn in pastels. The piece was abstract and I had inscribed three words: "Divine" at the bottom; "Support" at the top; and in the middle I had written "Rebirth". This last word took my attention.

As I admired my work, smiling to myself because I was so surprised at how creative I had become, I noticed that someone had come along and played with the drawing, smudging some areas and adding another colour from the chalk dust on the easel.

At first I was a little horrified and immediately started trying to fix it up. But amid the fear driven by loss, and some annoyance towards the child that was in my room earlier that day, I stopped to take in the added colours. A smile slowly spread across my face when I saw that the colour was orange. To me, this meant balance, creativity, and empowerment, moving through and accepting change. I breathed out a sigh. The other colour was yellow — new beginnings, warmth and the higher source for this time in our evolution. I no longer feared. I surrendered to this wonderful learning experience and I felt a beautiful warm connection to this child who had innocently played with my drawing — thank you for being my teacher: and another light to show me the way.

8th January 2011

Channelling: Seeing through the eyes of your heart truly gives you a real view of your inner and outer world. Seeing through the eyes of your heart connects you to a greater, more encompassing view. This is different from what you see through your eyes, which are limited. You are taught from a very young age to view through your eyes only. This is a car, this is daddy, and this is Billy the dog. It is the way you teach children how to see. Yet you take away their natural gift of seeing through the heart, which connects them to all that is. All that is, is far more than the limited five senses that you have chosen. You even separate these senses, yet the knowing is connected to whatever is, was and will be. This is accessed through your heart, not your head. Intellect is not thought; it is energy flowing and forming through expression of the Source, the truth of life being continuous, a never-ending energy source. Unlimited and free.

Due to the vibration of the cells in your physical body you do not have the full potential of Source to flow through you and reside within you. As you elevate and connect through the heart energy you lose the need to give the ego full attention. Through this, you understand to not live in fear and separation. You feel the flow of love moving within and through you, and through this you accomplish nirvana. Yet this often is temporary at first, for you are still feeding into the grid created to keep you in a state of separation and fear. So you stop believing! You stop knowing!

You remain disconnected from your truth and your full potential as a Light Being, transforming the density of the human being into so much more! If you were to view the world as we see it, you would see shadow and darkness with many beautiful lights similar to how you would view the stars lit up against a dark night sky.

So many of you are breaking through the darkness and seeing the light. So many of you are connecting to the stillness within. So many of you are disconnecting from your thoughts to know the truth of our world.

Yes, our world. You do not have to leave the human body to find what you call heaven. You do not have to leave the human body to come HOME! You have never left. This is an illusion created by ego and the misconception created by those few who wish to hold the power. Yet you embrace the power race like a child wanting their parent's love and protection.

11th January 2011

Channelling: Early in the morning everyone is sleeping, yet we never sleep. We continue to teach you through the grace and great Universal Ribbon of Light. We download information so that you shall integrate it and share it with your world. Many of you are receiving this information at once. Many of you have the ability and knowledge to share. Many of you will share this information even unknowingly, with others. Through your actions, your responses and the energy flow within your words, there is so much learning continuing on a large scale. You have so much Universal knowledge available to you NOW! Do you always understand your responses in a situation? Do you wonder sometimes, where did that sentence come from? That was so profound and how did I know that information? Many of you ponder and accept gratefully the information and wise words coming from your mouth that you share with another. Others will notice and then ignore, continuing as they had been, almost unaware of the gift in that moment.

Maria: Why do we download from the Library of Knowledge whilst we sleep?

Channelling: Because we are protecting you from destroying your race and the Earth. This life is a gift and so many of you have lost your connection - your inner knowing, with the ability and understanding to create a magnificent world filled with happiness and harmony. Every living thing on this planet works together in synchronicity to support, nurture and create.

Yes I can see your thoughts. Limitation, limitation, limitation. Don't you believe the stories about Adam and Eve? Living in complete harmony on Earth? There is truth to this. Yet the snake enticing Eve to eat the apple is symbolic of your ego and free will wanting power over you. The snake is the will, the apple is the sweetness promised. Yet, once you take that bite you cannot forget the taste of the perfect sweetness and you want more and more and more. An emotion is born. Power over an aspect within you, and an addiction — a need, a thirst, a hunger. Yet see how you separated yourself from the *whole* then quickly created many more aspects of the self and drew yourselves further away from your truth and real power – Love.

13th January 2011

Channelling: Travelling is seeing sight through thought. Many believe that to love is to allow yourself to be connected to another. To love is a small aspect. For, when you connect through love, it creates love. So many choose to travel through the thought process even though it is a false reality created through distance. Many choose to see through the eyes of thought, yet thought has no eyes. You believe thought has the vision into the future. Why do you put so much effort into this form of travel? Why not flow through the light of love and allow it to show you the way. Allow your understanding to be based in the reality of what you are. For love is surely an enlightened experience to connect to.

Valleys flow throughout your system. You are an exact replica of Mother Earth. Listen. Really feel this energy of what we share. See yourself as you see Mother Earth. See the energy surrounding Mother Earth. The Earth has an energy unlike any other planet. This is why you are able to exist as you are. Your physical body is in tune with the Earth's same energy field. Together you co-exist. Every plant, animal, insect, mammal has the same energy field. For this is all part of the co-existence, the reality of being on this star.

You ask how you were created, yet you don't see the obvious that has always been there. Many of your scientists today are understanding this more and more as they are willing to forgo their many centuries of conditioning. This Earth cannot exist without you and you cannot exist without the Earth.

25th January 2011

Channelling: To choose love is to live a life free of fear. To choose love is to see only through love. When the Universe was in its early days, there was only a darkness never seen before and possibly never to be seen again. Through this darkness, much came into existence. Then came the first light. Light was created to balance the darkness. Then came many lights, which were seen to be stars existing as a paradigm, through which light streams were created, and through this existed life. Not as you experience or understand. Life existed only through the existence of everything else. You see, this was the beginning of the Universe in all its beauty and glory. How then do you say the planets were formed? How then were the life forms created in their uniqueness? Do you choose to open to the possibility that much more exists? How does the love shine so brightly yet you choose to smother it with your thoughts, doubts and fears? There is so much that we have shared over many thousands of years. There is so much that we continue to share, yet your race denies the simplest of examples!

Why do you choose to flow in fear? Why do you choose to disconnect from love? Only you can know and, even though we continue to guide, you deny your right to feel and believe in the Source within.

26th January 2011

Channelling: See you now. See you in this moment. Can you feel the anticipation of this moment? Can you allow the gift of this moment to draw breath within you? You, my child, are now listening. Hooray! Let this moment last a lifetime. Allow the sun to shine through you. Allow the gift to be long lasting. Know that this moment is a blessing. Thank you for taking the time to draw this moment into you, allowing you to be in a scene of colour and light for you are anticipating the moment in awe. Thank you, my child, for your attention. There are many moments like this one, even while your life appears lost as you look to the next moment without noticing the one you are in. We are not just talking about you, my child. We trust that others who are reading this will recognise themselves in this energy. Many say that nothing is lost because they can make up for the moment in the next, but understand the sense of compounded loss that is created on an unconscious level. This you grieve; then you add to the mix of guilt, sadness, anger, as you blame yourself or even others. Can you see where we are going? We know you now question how are you going to make up for the moments lost without carrying the loss and grief with you? You fear becoming overwhelmed at the size of the letting go.

How ridiculous, we hear some of you thinking, while others are in quiet contemplation. Can you understand why you are always searching? Why some of you feel there is a loss and you have forgotten something? This drains your life force. You rollercoaster from feeling energised to feeling drained. Can you understand the energy of separation throughout this time? What would you think if we told you that your soul purpose is to be in the moment, and recognise each moment as a whole, being connected and connecting? Not carrying what we call dense emotions — emotions whose only purpose is to drain and create fear, isolation and the recognition and confirmation of separateness. It would not be fair if we were to share this with you and not share the solution.

First recognise your feelings in this moment, you know these through the sensations in your body. Next choose to listen to what your mind is saying about those feelings. Really listen. Do you feel these thoughts and feelings are in fact love? Do you feel these thoughts and feelings support your connectedness to all that is? Do you really know what connection feels like? Do you remember feeling free? Do you remember feeling light? Do you remember completeness, love, bliss, calm? Lack of wanting? Lack of loss? Lack of searching? Lack of lack itself?

Through so many thoughts, do you come to any conclusions? Are you seeing a sequence flowing through? Are you understanding the energy of life when you experience the gift of love, which is your only true state of being? You will understand there are no limitations or fear. You, Maria, are smiling. Can you feel the energy flow within? Can you sense the energy flowing through you and connecting you to your surroundings?

I sat on top of a mountain near Warburton, surrounded by Australian bush. The clouds rolled past. It was just past midday. The sky was grey, the air cool, yet comfortable. Amid the peace, the birds and insects were happily singing. Strangers had just walked by with their dogs — their laughter and chatter complemented the ambience. When they had left, all was quiet again.

6th February 2011

Channelling: Seeing the light within your world will allow you to remove all darkness within. There are so many reasons to live in the darkness, fear, sadness, regret, anger, disappointment. Yet to see the light within you and to connect to the warmth of love, will fill the emptiness that the dark emotions create.

Maria: Okay I understand that we can bridge the darkness by drawing in the loving kind thoughts and actions of others towards us. In other words, when I couldn't get in touch with the love to support and lift me from within, when I was so tired and drained, you gave me the vision of the many thank you cards, kind words and gratitude from my students and clients. It helped me connect to that energy, allowing it to penetrate and really fill me. Before, it was as if my protective shield and lack of worthiness had banked it up and not allowed the energy to penetrate, yet when I really connected to that love and consciously accepted it, the banks burst and flowed into me. Thank you.

Channelling: As we continue, we realise there is more that we know, yet so much more for each of you to learn. Consider this: if you had all of the money and security you required, could you possibly allow yourself to be free to flow with your inner knowing, to be happy, and lead from fullness rather than emptiness and fear? There are many who have this "security" but cannot and will not allow themselves to be free to live. What comes first: the chicken or the egg? If you want to create happiness you must believe that you can create happiness. Know you must look within to connect to the love energy that resides like a stream of endless light connecting you to all that is, and what will be. This connection knows no limitations, no conditions. This stream is endless through so many ways of being. Love has no conditions. It just is. Love is life. Life is love. So live love and love to live. Many generations follow the paths set behind them, yet do not choose to connect to the path they are standing on and do not look forward. What if you did not know your family history? What if you forgot the past and only remembered the present moment? Would you see this as an opportunity to discover, adventure, walk forward? You would not carry the negative emotions that create the darkness within, for you wouldn't remember those experiences. You would know love, for it is your greatest ally. You would know life because nature shares it with you. You would know light because every human has a spirit that shines through them. You would be with Oneness, content in life. So, you see, if you were not afraid of living and you did not carry the darkness and emptiness within you. You would Stop Looking!

Through this connection with the Guardians of the Light I have come to understand that life is forever evolving. It will lead us to see clearly from a different perspective. We might stand at the top of a mountain. It might shape us into an eagle where our wings lift us into freedom of flight. We could end up in the middle: a volcano feeling the depths of despair, with emotions that rumble and flare. Either way, my spirit has chosen to be here on this Earth, and I will learn to be more present, more conscious, so that I may experience the delights, the abundance, and feel with every breath I take.

I will skip like a stone thrown across the water, and I will dive into the greater depths of the unknown. The adventure is in the discovering. It stimulates every cell within me to be all that I can be.

From this day forth I will show love, compassion and kindness to me. I trust that the ripple effect will be felt by thee.

I know and trust that we are guided. We are not alone. xx

Notes

Notes

www.ingramcontent.com/pod-product-compliance
Lightning Source LLC
Chambersburg PA
CBHW071445090426
42737CB00011B/1779